MODERN
RUSSIAN
POETRY

D1258196

Modern Russian Poetry

TRANSLATED AND EDITED BY
OLGA ANDREYEV CARLISLE
AND ROSE STYRON

The Viking Press   New York

For Michael and Susanna

We should like to express our gratitude to Olga and Vadim Andreyev, Professor Rose Raskin, Henry Carlisle, and Professor Merle Feinsod for their generous contributions to this project. Our thanks go also to our editor, Velma Varner, whose encouragement and patience were invaluable.

ACKNOWLEDGMENTS

Acknowledgment is made to the following publishers and authors or their representatives for their permission to use previously published material. Every reasonable effort has been made to clear the use of the poems in this volume with the copyright owners. If notified of any omissions, the editors and publisher will gladly make the proper corrections in future editions.

"A Ballad About Nuggets" by Yevgeny Yevtushenko, translated by John Updike, was first published in *Life* magazine, February 17, 1967. Copyright © 1967 by John Updike.

Excerpt from "Stalin" by Osip Mandelstam, translated by Robert Lowell, reprinted with permission from *The New York Review of Books*. Copyright © 1965 by Robert Lowell.

"Pages from a Tashkent Diary" from *Vogue*, copyright © 1969 by The Condé Nast Publications Inc.

Selections from *Voices in the Snow* copyright © 1962 by Olga Andreyev Carlisle. Selections from *Poets on Street Corners* by Olga Carlisle, copyright © 1968 by Random House, Inc. Reprinted by permission of Random House, Inc.

PICTURE CREDITS

Grateful acknowledgment is made to the following persons who supplied photographs: Mme. Bonneau-Lafitte, from the New York Public Library Picture Collection, 190; Michael V. Carlisle, 85 (upper left); Inge Morath (© Magnum Photos), 22, 44; Mark Slonim, 128; *Novosti* from Sovfoto, 82 (upper left and right), 84 (upper right); and to Olga Andreyev Carlisle for the photographs on pages 34, 62, 82 (bottom), 84 (upper left and bottom), 85 (upper and lower right), 104, 142, 162, and 178.

CONTENTS

INTRODUCTION

The Soviet Union is the largest country in the world. A federation of fifteen republics, it stretches from the eastern reaches of Europe to the Pacific Ocean. Russia is greatest in area and by far the most influential of these republics, and Russian is spoken everywhere in the Soviet Union. Everywhere, Russian culture dominates. The diverse nationalities which form the Union of the Soviet Socialist Republics since the Communist party took power in 1917, as well as those the USSR annexed after World War II, all have their own language and literature, but these are studied locally. One of the fifteen Soviet Republics, Georgia, has a considerable influence on Russia in the realm which interests us, poetry.

Ancient Russia was christianized in the tenth century. It was linked not with Rome but with the Eastern, or Greek, Orthodox Church of Constantinople, or Byzantium. This, together with Russia's remote geographic situation, contributed to the country's isolation from the rest of Europe.

9

In the Middle Ages, Russia was divided into numerous small principalities, called *knyazhestvo*, which fought with each other constantly. They were politically unstable and militarily weak. Just as the humanizing influence of the Renaissance began to make itself felt in certain Russian cities like Kiev and Novgorod, the country was overrun by Mongol and Tartar tribes from Asia.

Russia remained under the control of the invaders for almost three hundred years. The Tartar yoke, which was most oppressive, left marks on the Russian national character: it made the Russian masses submissive in the face of authority. Thus, in the late 1920s a ruthless dictator, Joseph Stalin, was able to dominate the USSR completely. Unchallenged for almost twenty-five years, he ruled with the help of a colossal secret-police force. Today the country is run by the Communist party, which enforces an extremely bureaucratic version of socialism in the Soviet Union. Like the Czechoslovakians before they were overrun in 1968, many Soviet citizens are yearning for "a Communism with a human face" which would respect their individual rights and needs while giving them the freedom to work for their country in the way they themselves see fit. However, there is no way such people can effectively fight for their views. Nor does there appear to be any immediate prospect of political change in Russia.

The Russian alphabet was invented in the ninth century by two Greek scholars from Salonica, St. Cyril and St. Methodius. It derives from the Greek one and is known as the Cyrillic alphabet. The earliest Russian writings were religious—prayers, sermons, and the lives of the saints, which were especially popular in Rus, as Russia was known in the Middle Ages. These liturgies were written in a language we now call Old Church Slavonic. Beloved also were fairy tales and folk poems circulating orally in the vernacular. For centuries, telling them was an important form of entertainment for the people of Russia.

Russian folklore has a distinct flavor. It is elaborate in style and remarkably rich in content. It stems in part from the country's pagan past. Russian folk tales often deal with the supernatural. Or else they recount the astonishing adventures of a poor young peasant, usually called Ivan. Ivan is said to be a simpleton, but he succeeds in outsmarting the authorities. He always marries the beautiful princess at the end. These stories helped form and enrich the Russian language. They served as an inspiration for the first great Russian poet, Alexander Pushkin (1799–1837).

Many influences met to create the new literary language which was born with Pushkin—Russian folklore, Slavonic liturgy, Baroque influences from Poland and Germany, and of course French classicism. French was the language of the Russian Imperial Court from the eighteenth century. At that time Russia was an aggressive, expanding empire. It was ruled by absolute monarchs known as czars—from the Latin *Caesar*—established first in Moscow and then in St. Petersburg (renamed Leningrad after the 1917 Revolution for the great Bolshevik leader, Vladimir Ilyich Lenin). Under Peter the Great Russia was forsaking the secular ways of old Rus. Acting with great harshness, the czars modeled Russian institutions on the pattern of the European states of the day. Thus, grammar and Russian prosody

11

as we know them today were first created in the seventeenth century, an adaptation of European classic standards to the Russian vernacular.

Pushkin was the most brilliant literary figure of a period known as the Russian Golden Age, which lasted roughly from 1810 till the middle of the nineteenth century. A great number of marvelous poets, all different from one other, were active then. The best known are Derzharin, Krylov, Zhukovsky, Griboyedov, Baratynsky, Yazykov, Tyutchev, and Lermontov—but there were many other remarkably talented writers in those years. Pushkin and his contemporaries had in common a great love for Russia and a compassion for its people—the eighteenth century, the so-called Age of Enlightenment, had not improved their lot. On the contrary, under Peter the Great (1672–1725) and Catherine II, the Great (1729–1796), military conscription and heavy taxes levied in order to finance many grandiose building projects, such as Peter's creation of an opulent new capital—St. Petersburg (built in a swampy isolated region on the Baltic Sea)—made their lives progressively more miserable. Catherine had canceled all civil rights for the huge population of Russian serfs, and under her reign serfdom was codified in Russia. Alarmed by the extreme poverty of the peasants, Pushkin and the writers who followed him never lost sight of the fate of the Russian people, though many of these writers were of aristocratic origin themselves, benefiting by the institution of serfdom.

The history of Russian literature shows that great art is usually the expression of a whole country's deepest concern. In the nineteenth century Russia gave the world two great novelists. Leo Tolstoy (1828–1910), the author of *War*

12

and Peace, and Fyodor Dostoyevsky (1821–1881) were deeply involved with the daily life of the Russian people. As for poetry, ever since the days of Pushkin it has been an ideal means of communication for an oppressed people, more gifted for lyric and verbal expression than for the visual arts, though Russian medieval icon painting and architecture are beautiful and quite original despite their dependence on the artistic traditions of Byzantium.

In the nineteenth century, love of poetry grew very quickly in Russia, much more quickly than literacy. In 1837 tens of thousands of people payed homage to Pushkin as his body was lying in his St. Petersburg house. He had been victim of a duel which was apparently staged by the czar in order to rid Russia of an influential, freedom-loving public figure. Among the mourners, only a very few could read, but Pushkin's name, his love of liberty, and the echoes of some of his poems had already entered the Russian popular conscience. Pushkin had a reputation as an atheist, but a deeply religious people nonetheless sensed that the poet had been one of their purest, most eloquent spokesmen.

Throughout their country's history, the great majority of Russian poets protested against the tyranny which, in one form or another, has always prevailed in Russia. But no government can stifle the extraordinary popularity of poetry in Russia. Andrei Voznesensky, a young poet who is widely published in the USSR, said not long ago: "The popularity of poetry in the USSR demonstrates that, today, Communists are interested also in the life of the spirit—and not only in materialistic concepts. For us, poetry is a shared experience. Poets create in solitude, but when they

13

read their works to crowds of listeners, the poet and his public commune. They experience together something new and deep. . . ."

In the USSR in the last decade there have been readings when tens of thousands of listeners assembled in huge stadiums to hear poets recite their works. These events, like the one held in the Luzhniki Stadium in Moscow in 1961, were so electrifying that the government has subsequently forbidden literary gatherings of this size. Nonetheless, smaller poetry readings are still often held in the USSR. A whole country, deprived of spiritual outlets such as religion (which is discouraged by the Communist party), is looking for the "life of the spirit" through poetry.

During a conversation I had with him in Moscow in the early sixties, the flamboyant young poet Yevgeny Yevtushenko, Voznesensky's contemporary and one of Russia's best-known writers, told me how the first outdoor public poetry reading, now a yearly event in Moscow, had taken place in 1955:

In October of that year, a group of young poets organized a sale of inscribed books at one of Moscow's larger bookstores. Spontaneously a crowd gathered. Before long, several hundred people stood outside the store. On the spur of the moment and despite the cold weather, the poets carried makeshift tables out of doors and sold their books to "a thousand hands," as Yevtushenko described it. When their books were sold out, the poets climbed in turn on the tables and read their poems. Evening neared and snowflakes began to fall but for hours the crowd stood in the street and listened. Since then, an afternoon of public reading and of selling books has become a tradition in Moscow in the fall—and a symbol of new times.

Then Yevtushenko spoke of the birth of a new intelligentsia in the USSR. "It is like trying to catch a flow of water in the palm of your hand," he said. "Most of it flows out but a little is retained in the cup of the hand. This is happening now. We and our children will

14

eventually retain this little amount of water as against the main stream—but of course the ever increasing main stream is our first concern. The fact that the Soviet government has been able to open the world of good books to the masses of people gives us faith in the future of Russia."*

It is hard for us outside the USSR to assess exactly the scope and significance of poetry's extreme popularity there. Andrei Voznesensky and Yevgeny Yevtushenko are official poets, often disagreeing with the authorities, sometimes challenging them, but never clashing openly with them. Tens of thousands of copies of their works are published every year. These poets are as popular there as movie stars are in the West. They enjoy a standard of living which is equaled only by that of highly placed party members. But there are dozens of nonofficial poets throughout the USSR. They may be completely unknown outside a small circle of friends, because their verse does not conform to the requirements of the official literary doctrine of the Soviet Union, known as Social Realism.† This is a frustrating situation for the student of modern Russian literature—as it is for the poets themselves or their would-be public. For example, the poet Joseph Brodsky gained literary recognition by accident. Had he not been the victim of a highly publicized trial, his writings, excellent as they are, might well still be unknown to us today.

One of the great moments of Russian literature was the Revolution of 1917. In the years just preceding and fol-

---

*Olga Andreyev Carlisle, *Voices in the Snow* (New York: Random House, 1962), pp. 84–85.

† The writer Maxim Gorki is credited with inventing this term, which met with Stalin's approval. The doctrine it refers to is an endorsement of realism to the exclusion of all other artistic styles. Although it is not always strictly enforced, this doctrine was never repealed, and it is (always) there to put down writers with modernistic tendencies.

lowing it, a poetic surge of almost Elizabethan scope engulfed Russia. These years may be compared to Pushkin's age: the same passionate readership, the same exalted role assigned to the poets by the reading public, the same hopes for social and political changes. Among the ten or twelve great poets who wrote at that time, Blok, Pasternak, Akhmatova, Tsvetayeva, Mandelstam, Yesenin, and Mayakovsky may be singled out. (The other poets of that period, left out of this book partly because of translation problems, are Innokenty Annensky, Fyodor Sologub, Vyacheslav Ivanov, Maximilian Voloshin, Andrei Bely, Velemir Khlebnikov, Nikolai Gumilev, and Vladislav Khodasevich.) Except for Mayakovsky—who was a public figure identified with the Soviet government—these poets upheld the tradition of compassion and humanism which had been created in Russia by the great nineteenth-century writers. The poets of Revolution were devoted to their country, but this did not blind them to the rest of the world. They loved freedom. They were hopeful about the Revolution. Above all, they had been revolutionary in their writings. Mandelstam and Pasternak had revolutionized the world of poetic perceptions, breaking away from nineteenth-century intellectual and psychological concepts. Tsvetayeva and Mayakovsky had created new, daring rhythms. As for Anna Akhmatova, a traditionalist in terms of form, her innovating spirit is to be found in the realm of sentiment. She taught herself, and all of Russian womanhood—for her popularity in Russia was immense in the twenties and again in the sixties—to shed the coy Victorian attitudes of the past in order to find inner freedom.

16

There are many young poets writing in Russia today—Yevgeny Yevtushenko, Andrei Vosnesensky, Bella Akhmadulina, Joseph Brodsky, Robert Rozhdestvensky, Rimma Kozakova, Novella Matoyeva, Yuna Moritz, Victor Sosnora, Vadim Kushner, and others—but none may yet be compared in importance to Blok or Pasternak. Pasternak himself had this to say on the subject during a talk we had in his house in Peredelkino in 1960, while I was under the spell of my recent discovery of Yevtushenko and Akhmadulina—of their works and of their friendship:

> Today's poetry is often rather ordinary. It is like the pattern on a wallpaper, pleasant enough but without real raison d'etre. Of course some young people show talent. Yevtushenko, for example. However . . . I believe that prose is today's medium, elaborate, rich prose like that of Faulkner. Today's work must re-create whole segments of life.*

Possibly, Pasternak, the author of *Doctor Zhivago,* was right: The most important literary statement to come out of Russia in the sixties was made in prose by Alexander Solzhenitsyn. He is a poet turned prose writer, and his impassioned, monumental novels, *The First Circle* and *The Cancer Ward,* have become international best sellers. However, real appreciation for poetry lives on in the USSR. A high level of poetic culture exists there despite Stalinist persecutions which destroyed many poets, and the present policy of tight governmental censorship. For in the Soviet Union everything that is published—books, magazines, newspapers—is government controlled.

Those books which are acceptable for publication are relatively inexpensive; they are sold in bookstores, or even from outdoor makeshift stalls set in the streets of the cities.

---

*Carlisle, *Voices in the Snow,* p. 200.

17

Russians love to read; people of all ages and all walks of life line up to buy newly printed books—and most sought after are books of poetry. In fact, those by fashionable poets like Voznesensky or Yevtushenko are extremely hard to obtain. Though they are usually published in huge printings (editions of several hundred thousand volumes are not unusual for "official" writers), they are in such demand that they often disappear in one day. Thus many poems—unpublished or out of print—circulate only in *samizdat,* as the system of typing and passing manuscripts around is known in the Soviet Union. (*Samizdat* means, literally, "self-publication.")

Indeed, poetry is the art which suffers least from censorship. Often *samizdat* is not even necessary for the distribution of poems. They circulate orally with great ease wherever people have trained memories for remembering verse—and Russians, with their tradition of story telling and poetry reciting, are remarkable in this respect. Thus, the poems of the Russian classics as well as those of poets banned by Stalin circulated in the depths of the Russian concentration camps during Stalin's regime. In the nineteenth century, a whole new folkloric tradition was revived—that of the thieves' ballads, known in Russia as *blatnoi.* Nowadays, these are composed by poets who adopted the *blatnoi* style. These ballads are bitter and even sometimes obscene, but they are nonetheless often highly poetic. Today, along with the poems of Akhmatova and Mandelstam, these ballads are great favorites among the more sophisticated young people of Russia.

On the whole, Russian readers want to be entertained outside the limits set for them by the government. Many are trying to come to terms with their own consciences. They have never been told that they as a nation shared in the guilt of Stalin's crimes; they are discouraged even from thinking about them. But the past with its fantastic, secret horrors haunts them nonetheless: Who is responsible for the deaths of millions in camps?

And good poetry speaks only the truth. It is the voice of one individual rather than that of the collective—yet it is also a means of communing with others, as Voznesensky pointed out. Poetry can alleviate the sense of anguish and doubt which to some degree is always part of the human condition, especially if a government denies the legitimacy of such feelings.

Traditionally, anthologies present a wide sampling from a given field, with a great number of writers represented by a short fragment or a couple of poems each. Instead, we have studied in depth a smaller number of authors. The poets included in this anthology are, in our opinion, likely to endure in the history of Russian literature. Moreover, they have at the present time an enormous influence on their contemporaries. Every poem presented in this book is well known in the USSR. Another consideration in our choosing this format is purely practical. We favor the important modern Russian poets because only first-rate poetry translates well, coming through in another language in a striking, fresh manner. Of course, a great poet can take an indifferent foreign poem and turn it into a *chef-d'oeuvre* in his own tongue—but his rendition is likely to have only a remote connection with the original. An indifferent poem is usually a banal one—and banality is international, equally boring in all languages. Often, and most poets agree, a free adaptation of the original is the most effective approach to translating. To emphasize our attempt at capturing what is relevant in Russia today, the poets are arranged in reverse chronological order. Despite the popularity of the poets of the Revolutionary period, many of whom remained unpublished for decades under Stalin and are now being rediscovered in the USSR, the Russian reader is most attentive to young voices, listening for strains of a new greatness.

Chapter 5 of this book, incorporating nine poets' work into one sequence, is a kind of anthology within an anthology, aimed at recapturing the continuity of Russian poetry in the face of history's upheavals. Literature is above all the creation of extraordinary individuals whose powers of imagination astonish us. No one but Pasternak would have a swing reflected in a mirror on a summer day, where:

> Inside the room the huge garden carouses,
> raises a fist at the mirror to harass,
> runs to the moving swing, catches and clouds it,
> and shakes that fist, and does not break the
> glass.

To a Russian reader, this is, inimitably, Pasternak's vision. It is childlike yet refined, intellectual yet sensuous, reminiscent of Matisse's flat paintings, which suggest a whole other world, rich and third dimensional. But literature is also continuity, a slow fruition, a growth over many decades. Artists of intense individuality may have a destructive effect on their followers, like Mayakovsky, whose poetic voice, misleadingly easy to imitate, resulted in

20

numbers of versifiers who, having nothing to say, all sound like Mayakovsky. Good traditional writers are the ones who carry on certain literary traditions, helping literature survive from generation to generation.

—Olga Andreyev Carlisle

Inge Morath (© Magnum Photos)

JOSEPH BRODSKY

1940—

$\mathcal{J}$oseph Brodsky, born in 1940, is the most important young poet in Leningrad today. A friend of Anna Akhmatova before her death, he carries on her civilized, erudite literary tradition. And like the young Akhmatova, Brodsky is a marvelous guide to his native city. During a long leisurely evening walk he will conjure up the spirits of Pushkin, Dostoyevsky, and Blok with every step.

In 1964 Brodsky was the victim of a scandalous political trial. He was accused of "social parasitism" by the local Leningrad authorities because he had no steady job and earned his living translating poetry from English and Spanish. He was sent out of Leningrad to work on a collective farm. For many months, he shoveled manure near Archangel in the north of Russia.

The Soviet intelligentsia was outraged by Brodsky's trial, a deliberate attempt to discredit nonconforming writers in the USSR, and so was the West. Pressures mounted, and eventually the Soviet authorities released Brodsky, allowing

23

him to return to Leningrad where he now lives modestly but in peace.

Brodsky is an intensely original poet. He is a great admirer of the American poets Edwin Arlington Robinson and Robert Frost. His knowledge of contemporary American poetry and also of classical English literature clearly has helped to shape him. At present, while writing a great deal of new verse, he is engaged in translating John Donne into Russian for one of the state-run Soviet publishing houses.

Brodsky's writings are lyric, and sometimes rather hermetic. He has used surrealistic devices, such as the enumeration of household items in his "Great Elegy for John Donne." The intrusion of daily trivia into his poetry relates him to the American pop artists. He has a Gogolian sense of the grotesque. Brodsky's poems often have strong religious overtones, echoing that muted interest in religion spreading throughout the Soviet Union. Although seldom published in his own country, the works of Joseph Brodsky are well known in literary circles today.

Olga Carlisle met Brodsky for the first time in the spring of 1967 at the house of Nadezhda Mandelstam, the widow of the great poet of the thirties, while the young Leningrad writer was visiting Moscow briefly. Here is her report of the evening: Mrs. Mandelstam—using the English expression with a certain amused pleasure—had warned me that Joseph Brodsky was "a charming, but very contrary young man. It is shyness," she said. "He is a poet and needs readers; his haughtiness is a pose. I hold him in great esteem. And of course Anna Andreyevna (Akhmatova) thought him to be the most talented of all our young poets."

On the appointed evening, after supper, a few friends sat around the table in Mrs. Mandelstam's small but cozy kitchen. In those years when the hopes for a thaw in Soviet cultural matters were still running high, this kitchen was Moscow's most stimulating salon. Writers, scientists, painters gathered there in the evening for tea and conversation. A brilliant conversationalist with a sharp tongue, Nadezhda Mandelstam attracts the best minds of Moscow, creating an atmosphere of gaiety and informality, encouraging a free exchange of ideas. Her special talent is an ability to get involved with "living art," to take risks in her judgments, to seek out tirelessly people who have something new to say, rather than those who have a safely established literary reputation.

Despite the delicious tea dispensed from the kitchen stove by a young woman physicist, a friend of our hostess, the evening started inauspiciously. Brodsky was distant and brooding. He was silent at first. When the conversation turned to politics he started defending those positions which, he knew, Mrs. Mandelstam and her guests were certain to condemn. . . . Interrupting a conversation which threatened to become unpleasant, Mrs. Mandelstam asked Joseph Brodsky to read aloud some poems; and a remarkable transformation took place in the small kitchen, similar to the magic which unfolds when a good pianist sits at the piano during an otherwise conventional social occasion, and the seldom-used grand piano in the drawing room suddenly comes to life. Brodsky stood up and recited

25

a poem which he had recently written. He was addressing his own poems:

> In my desk
> they do not want to sleep,
> because they are alive
> —and to be buried
> alive is torture.
> And so we part.
> You, poems, go to the people
> while I go
> where all people
> end.

As he read, the moody dark-eyed young man with a receding hairline and a bored expression on his fine-featured sensitive face became an inspired being who had the power of total communication with other people. He was reciting from memory in a strangely nasal singsong fashion, emphasizing the sounds rather than the meaning of his verse. The reading became frenzied as he recited parts of his "Great Elegy for John Donne." The enumeration of everyday objects, building to some kind of mysterious crescendo—perhaps a poet's wild attempt to catalogue *all* of the Lord's creations—was overwhelming. As Brodsky finished the elegy and sat down, all uneasiness had vanished from Mrs. Mandelstam's kitchen. We were all Russians united by our common love of poetry. Nothing else mattered.

Great Elegy for John Donne

Listen! John Donne
has fallen asleep
and all around him, fallen asleep:
the walls of his room
the steps of a staircase,
floors, tables, clocks and old glass-
ware, bottles, and porcelain
crockery, crystal,
breadknife and fresh-baked loaves, all still.
Night is everywhere, everywhere night,
in corners and eyes,
in papers in the drawer,
in next week's sermon, her words, and there
in the garden,
in fire tongs and bellows,
each careless thing: a waistcoat, the shadows,
behind the mirror and
washbowl and bed,
the crucifix, the broom against the door.
All are asleep, asleep, asleep . . .
See, through the window
white snow whirls on
sloping roofs—the whole neighborhood
sleeps, cut off by the
guillotine
of the window's sash, the arches of stone,
the walls, grills.
Light will not flare
nor a wheel scrape nor a whisper flurry.

27

No silk-soft noise. Only the snow cries.
Everything sleeps.
No dawn reflects
the prisons and the castles sleeping
the scales of the fishmarket,
dogs on leashes,
cats in the cellar with still-pointed ears.
London's asleep.
A sail in her harbor
under its bow churns snow and water
blurring soft
into the distant sky.

Listen! John Donne
has gone to sleep
and the sea is asleep and the chalky cliffs—
the whole island is seized with the same
slumber. Each garden is closed
with a triple latch; maples and pines and
crabs and wolves and
foxes drowse,
the bear has crawled into his dream
and the snow piles up outside his lair
and the birds are still, the crows, still,
the English space is quiet.
A star sparkles. All the dead
lie in their coffins quietly sleeping
and in their beds the living sleep
in the seas of their nightshirts,
each alone, embracing. . . .

But hark!—in the cold darkness
someone comes weeping—
someone afraid in the power of winter. . . .
Gabriel, Gabriel, surely it's you,
alone in the midst of winter,
your trumpet sobbing.
No, It is I,
your soul, John Donne.
Here alone on the heights of heaven
I brood, my senses heavy as chains. . . .
everything dreams in a proud exhaustion,
and God is only a light in the window
of the house most distant
on a foggy night.
The fields are here
but all unplowed,
the years and the centuries, all unplowed.
Only the woods
stand like a wall and only the rains
dance in gigantic grass.

That first woodsman, whose skinny horse wandering
into the strange thicket pawed with fear,
climbs up a pine tree and sees the blaze
of light in his own far valley.
Near him, the world is vague.
His tranquil glance glides over distant roofs.
Here in the quiet light
no sound comes
of a dog's barking, a church bell's song.

Soon he will fathom that all of life
is far away, and toward the deep woods
brusquely he'll turn his horse.
At once the reins the sled the dark the fleshless
horse and even he
fade to a Biblical dream.

Here I weep
And there's no way out.
Must I again be part of these stones
and only dead be allowed
to fly up there?
I'll be alone in the humid earth
and I'll forget you, my light, forever,
forget to follow that fruitless desire:
the joining of flesh and spirit.
And while I weep, troubling your rest,
the snow in the dark unmelting flies
and sews up our separation.
Back and forth the needle flies.
No, it's not I but you,
John Donne, weeping.
You lie alone; the crockery sleeps
in the cupboard; the snow flies
and falls on the sleeping house, and flies
into the dark out yonder.

Like a bird he sleeps in his nest
for he has entrusted to that fair star
now hidden by clouds his clear ways,
his thirst for a purer life.

Like a bird's his soul is clean
though the world's ways are sin; they are more
natural than a crow's nest over the gray
masses of empty birdhouses.
Like a bird he'll wake in the day,
but now sheer whiteness covers him
and the space between his soul and body
in sewn with snow and sleep.
All the world
has fallen asleep.
A few lines still wait for their endings:
"Worldly love is only a singer's homage,
love of the spirit only an abbot's flesh."
"No matter which wheel catches the falling water,
the wheat it grinds will be the same wheat."
"One man may share his life with another,
but no one shares his death."
The cloth of the night sky frays and he
who wants may tear it from every side.
He leaves, and returns, and tears again,
and only the firmament, once in a dark while
picks up the tailor's needle.
Sleep, sleep, sleep John Donne.
Do not toss though your torn cloak droops.
Any moment, any hour
there yet may shine through cloud and blizzard
the star which all those years
your fair world blessed.

TRANSLATED BY ROSE STYRON AND OLGA CARLISLE

31

I

The great Hector was killed by arrows.
His soul is floating down the dark stream,
leaves rustling, and clouds darkening
and Andromache's distant weeping is barely heard.

On this evening of sorrow,
Ajax waded to his knees in the transparent brook.
Life was rushing out of his open eyes,
following Hector.
The warm water came up to his chest,
darkness filling
the bottomless eyes which searched waves and bushes.
The water was waist deep.
Seized by the stream,
lifted, his heavy sword
carried him away.

—1961
TRANSLATED BY OLGA CARLISLE

II

We live again by the bay and its waters,
and clouds pass us by, floating high.
A modern Vesuvius is raging here,
settling dust on the side streets,
windowpanes rattling,
ashes will cover us too.

At this pitiful hour,
to take a tram,

32

to travel to the city limits
and walk into your house.
Centuries hence
when a party of diggers
unearths our town
under a layer of ashes—
O, to be found
in your embrace.

—1962
TRANSLATED BY OLGA CARLISLE

BELLA
AKHMADULINA

1937—

Born and brought up in Moscow, Bella Akhmadulina is carrying on the dynamic literary tradition which flourished in Moscow in the Revolutionary years. Now in her early thirties, she is a skillful, passionate artist totally dedicated to her art. Her great loves are Tsvetayeva and Pasternak. Another is Georgia, Pasternak's beloved adopted land, which she often visits and which has inspired some of her most lyrical work:

> And God be witness,
> My dream about you, Georgia,
> is deep;
> A mountain gorge, or the valley
> of Allazanskaya.

TRANSLATED BY STANLEY NOYES
AND OLGA CARLISLE

Bella Akhmadulina's poetry is apolitical, and for this reason her works are only occasionally printed in the USSR—only two slim volumes of verse published to date.

The magazine *Yunost,* a widely circulated youth-oriented journal second only to *Novii mir* in literary excellence, has brought out a sizable part of her poetic output. Although they contain nothing politically subversive, some of her poems may only be obtained in typescript.

Seldom published as she may be, Bella Akhmadulina is a celebrity in the Soviet Union. She is extremely pretty and dresses elegantly. She first became well known in the late fifties when her husband, Yevgeny Yevtushenko, whom she later divorced but who is still a close friend, published a cycle of love poems dedicated to her. This had been a thrilling novelty after the several puritanical decades of Stalin's reign. Nowadays Akhmadulina has an important following for other reasons: she is one of the Soviet writers who champions intellectual freedom most uncompromisingly, and this makes her especially popular among the country's young people. Against the relatively drab background of Soviet daily life, Bella Akhmadulina's figure is one of glamour: the Soviet Union is the only country in the world where poetic achievement confers stardom.

Her poetry readings are extremely popular:

A sea of young people with ecstatic open faces; here and there middle-aged women in drab clothes, with gray faces, some with eyes filled with tears—they all press against one another on hard auditorium benches, trying to make room for those jammed in the aisles. Young men are precariously perched on window ledges halfway up to the ceiling; students are crowding to the very footlights of the brightly lit stage.

A pretty woman walks out onto the stage. She is wearing pumps with high heels. Her navy silk dress is extremely short, her reddish hair set according to the latest fashion. She looks like a doll with her heavily made-up wide-open dark eyes. She stands there a bit unsteadily, clutching the microphone, lifting an unseeing immobile face to the public. After six or seven outbursts of acclaim, she raises her left arm in a timid, rounded gesture—and perfect silence settles over the audience within seconds. Bella Akhmadulina is having a solo public reading for the first time in many months. This young woman, who was admitted into the Writers' Union as a translator rather than as a writer . . . is Russia's most famous young poetess. This evening at the Journalists' Club is one of the great events of the literary season in Moscow in the spring of 1967.

Akhmadulina recites her "Volcanoes" from memory, her eyes now almost closed, emphasizing the rhythm and assonances of her poem. Her voice is melodious and grieving. She seems on the verge of dissolving into tears as she addresses Pompei:

> What future did you assume,
> What were you thinking of and whom,
> When you leaned your elbow thus
> Thoughtlessly on Vesuvius?*

TRANSLATED BY W. H. AUDEN

New Blast Furnace
in the Kemerovo Metallurgical Combine

Up where the new blast furnace rises
and work goes on, a boy will dare
to laugh, to balance himself in the wind
as if he enjoyed life up there.

Nonchalantly he walks the ledge
even for that fleet instant or so
when his head perceives a dizzying,
a faint yearning for the ground below.

---

*Olga Andreyev Carlisle, *Poets on Street Corners* (New York: Random House, 1970), pp. 2–3.

37

He breathes freely, almost with joy,
though his irregular footsteps' echo jars,
and fire from his welding showers sparks
a cascade of falling August stars.

Oh, the ardor, the boundless daring!
and, suddenly, expectation found
that one of the girls who pass will measure
the space that yawns from him to the ground.

But girls are mysterious! One will stare
high up at him and not understand:
there is something she likes about it all
at a height he cannot command.

And yet on those rare occasions when
the circus comes, she'll turn quite pale
anxious as she strains to watch
the tightrope acrobat, lest he fail.

Without betraying his pique or hurt
he once again with an unconcerned air
looks down on the girls who've forgotten him
and scatters his sparks of fire.

—1959
TRANSLATED BY ROSE STYRON

38

Fifteen Boys

Fifteen boys, maybe more
maybe less
in apprehensive voices
tried me:
"Let's go to a movie, or the Museum of Fine Arts."
My answer, more or less:
"I really haven't time."
Fifteen boys presented me with snowdrops.
Fifteen boys in crushed voices
assured me:
"I'll never stop loving you."
My answer, more or less:
"We'll see."

Fifteen boys now live in peace.
They've fulfilled their weighty service
of snowdrops, letters, and despair.
Girls love them—
some much prettier,
others less pretty than I.
Fifteen boys with exaggerated airs
of ease, and sometimes gloating,
greet me when they pass,
when passing me they greet
their own liberation, routines of sleep and eating.

Last boy, you're coming to me in vain.
I'll place your snowdrops in a tumbler of water,
and their stocky stems

39

in silver bubbles will stand . . .
But you'll stop loving me, too—you'll see,
and becoming your own master,
you'll speak to me almost arrogantly
as if it were me you'd mastered
while down the street, the street, I walk away . . .

—1960

TRANSLATED BY ROSE STYRON AND OLGA CARLISLE

A Dream: I

Thunder is striking our house,
A blizzard wheels around us, a fire,
   a howling wheel.

   A howling fire,
it plays chords on the piano downstairs;
it is wounding my head.

O my sister, give me some ice. Midnight
has struck and sung its song.
O to cool down the dark gap in my mind!
The water is sharp with ice.

Like a last bridge my mind is burning,
cutting me off, an orphaned island.
   My sister, ice, to save me!
Some white, white ice!

40

My helpless mind is a huge machine
which rotates people and towns.
How to unwind this merry-go-round?
Give me some ice, some white, white ice!

I burn in a furnace, a Joan of Arc,
dogs barking, crowds whistling—I, so young!
Antarctic ice, be kind to me!

It was said afterward
that her throat was too small
for such a huge cry.

—1964
TRANSLATED BY OLGA CARLISLE

A Dream: II

It's all familiar,
the fall air, clear and sober,
the little house, the door half open,
the salty taste of our apples,

but a stranger is raking the garden.
He says he is the rightful owner now,
and asks me in. The brick floor, the blank
where the clock stood, that slant of light,

my rushed, uncertain steps,
my eyes that saw, and saw nothing,

41

your tender voices . . . but the gardener's wife
is standing there waiting.

"It's so foggy here! I lived here too, once,
a hundred years ago . . .
It's all the same, that same
smoky smell over the garden,

the dog's fur still wet on my fingers . . ."
"You don't say," the gardener answers,
cocking his head, coming closer.
Then he smiles, and asks,

"Isn't it you, though, that picture
up in the attic? Isn't it her,
with the long, old-fashioned bangs?
But your eyes have changed

since those terrible old days
a hundred years ago,
when you died, alone in the house here,
poor, without work or friends."

—1966

TRANSLATED BY JEAN VALENTINE AND OLGA CARLISLE

YEVGENY YEVTUSHENKO

1933—

Yevgeny Yevtushenko—Zhenya to his countless friends and admirers—is the most vital and energetic of Russia's young poets. He has been in the avant-garde of youth who demand that their nations be free and just, and he has taken great risks to speak out for human rights. Like his model Mayakovsky, to whom he is indebted for the effective declamatory style and bold colloquialisms of some of his verse, and with whom he shares a loathing for corruption and hypocrisy, Yevtushenko is a public figure involved with "the people." Yet his poems are stamped with individual sensitive responses to Russian history and landscapes, to contemporary events and newly discovered places, to poets and heroes, to women, to his own mercurial life.

If you have been a literary visitor to the USSR in the past few years, it is not unlikely that this tall handsome high-cheekboned young man with pale-blond hair and intense pale-blue eyes, who holds himself straight as a

45

matador poised to surprise you with a thrust of wit, a sparkle of mischief, has taken you in hand. If you were in Uzbekistan, say, early one sunny morning, he would have led you to the sprawling outdoor market, where lush ripe melons and fresh crusty bread provide a glorious breakfast, and natives of every corner of Asia pass by choosing brooms or bicycles or flowers while you and your host discuss art, humor, paper production, the necessity for patriotic Russians and Americans to understand each other. Or, late one evening, he would escort you to a secret garden behind a candlelit archway on the darkest, narrowest cobblestone street in Tashkent. Here a Moslem circumcision celebration would be in progress: old men seated apart on high, carpeted beds, guests arrayed at gay tables under the trees, children engaged in a joke-telling contest with a dwarf. The poet would drink to your health in the champagne he delights in, choose the tastiest of strange foods for you, and explain the exotic customs.

In Moscow, he would arrive by car from Peredelkino and with incredible generosity treat you to a personal Sunday. Nothing seems too much trouble: he will stop by at ancient log houses and a new glass shopping center, monasteries used by soldiers, and a shimmering church that rings with choral music, statued squares which honor Russia's writers, and marble monuments to Lenin, the studios of the best artists and his own Moscow flat—crammed with books in English (seven shelves of novels and poetry), photographs (his wife and young son, his friend El Cordobés), gifts from abroad, modern Russian sculpture and painting. Then, dinner at a restaurant actors frequent, an excellent play at the experimental Taganka

46

theater (Yesenin's *Pugachev*, perhaps), a trip upstairs afterward to talk with its director, Yuri Lubimov, and add your names to the ink scrawlings on the wall. Yevtushenko, who knows everyone, will identify the international signatures just as he identifies the local actor leaving the theater with the aloof blond he dubs "a frozen chicken." And he will describe with ardor the places you must visit next: Lake Baikal; the snowy taiga of his birthplace, Siberia.

Yevtushenko was born in 1933 in the quiet village of Zima, a stop on the trans-Siberian railroad. His peasant family was of mixed Russian, Ukrainian, and Tartar origin. His father was a geologist who once or twice took Zhenya on expeditions. They lived very modestly. As a small boy Zhenya was called upon to sing and dance, and he began to invent his own verses to set music to. The long vivid poem "Zima Junction," with its variety of folk and modern rhythms, documents this childhood, pays tribute to the family and colorful village life that formed it.

Separated from his family during the war, Yevtushenko came to Moscow and "slept under a staircase, living almost exclusively on sorrel leaves." His first poems were published at sixteen (in *Soviet Sport*—Zhenya is a confirmed sportsman), his first book at nineteen. He attended the Literary Institute but preferred writing to studying. Able to seize the moment and write with spontaneity, he emerged first as a prolific "newspaper poet." Then, his lyric talent maturing and his self-confidence expanding, he became a spokesman for youth. His voice and bearing, his flair for drama, made him a natural performer, and he attracted huge crowds at the outdoor poetry readings revived after Stalin's death.

In 1961 he read "Babi Yar" at that year's Day of Poetry. This poem, striking for both its intimate beauty and its brutal honesty, condemned anti-Semitism, a subject not openly discussed in the Soviet Union. In 1962 the famous "Heirs of Stalin," a frontal attack on the resurgence of Stalinism, appeared. In 1963 while he was abroad, Yevtushenko's *Precocious Autobiography* was published in the French paper *L'Express* without the permission of the Russian authorities. The poet was in trouble. His view of Stalin's legacy—poignantly illustrated by the scene of his funeral where onlookers were herded and crushed to death by police drivers who had "no instructions" to stop—and of certain mendacious bureaucrats whom he felt were once more betraying the Revolution, was hardly flattering. Aired in Paris, it brought venomous attacks at home, though until then Nikita Khrushchev had been his indulgent supporter. It was a time when pressure was being put on many artists and writers with liberal leanings to "confess" their ideological errors. Yevtushenko and Voznesensky found their public voices and freedom to travel suppressed.

After a time, the restrictions lifted. Zhenya, traveling alone or with his second wife Galya, was a favorite in Rome, New York, Mexico City, and Havana. He visited Africa and the Pacific ("Honolulu, you loll dreamily on your back in a silver-black nowhere . . ."), was exhilarated by an Alaska that felt like Siberia. He was nominated for the chair of poetry at Oxford. His good humor and optimism abounded, and he took criticism in his stride. Sometimes his pen seemed to have a light heart of its own:

Shuttling through time
                    like a train I go
from the city of Yes
                    to the city of No.
Like telephone wires
                    my nerves carry stress
from the city of No
                    to the city of Yes.
Love is expelled
                    from the city of No;
it looks like a room
                    upholstered in woe:
with bile every morning
                    they shine the parquet,
each object it polishes
                    scowls at the day.
The sofa,
            synthetic.
The walls,
            a mistake.
Is there a chance
            of good counsel
                    or flowers when I wake?
The answer to this
            as the carbons will show:
"No, no, no,
            no, no, no,
                    no, no, no, no . . ."
And when every light
            has been turned off to stay

49

the ghosts in the room
                    do a ghoulish ballet.
Though you buy your own
                    ticket,
                              what chance will you get
to leave for all time
                    the black city of Nyet?
In the city of Da
              life's birdsong is best,
a place without walls
                    it resembles a nest.
Every star of the sky
              asks to fall in your hand
and lips, any lips,
                    will await
                              your command.
There's no one to whisper,
                    "How silly this seems!"
and the mignonette
              begs you
                    to pluck it for dreams. . . .

TRANSLATED BY ROSE STYRON

Then, in 1968, he protested to his government by tele-
gram its invasion of Czechoslovakia. He was ashamed, he
said, to have his country desert the traditions of freedom
"upheld by Pushkin, Tolstoy, and Solzhenitsyn." Solzhenitsyn was being hounded because of his anti-Stalinist
novels. Now Yevtushenko was denied publication and his
place on the masthead of *Yunost* (*Youth*). His trips abroad
were curtailed, though Yevtushenko, like his friend

Voznesensky, has never severed his connections with the official world of Soviet Letters. At this time, there may be few authorized platforms for the Yevtushenkos of Russia to ascend, or afternoons like this one, even in the far reaches of middle Asia:

The hall was packed. Kids stood pressed together in the aisle clapping, cheering, wild with affection. We sat at the side of the stage, and looking down at the mass of eager young smiles I was reminded of the last time I had sat on a stage—when Senator Eugene McCarthy delivered a speech at the Cow Palace in San Francisco—the kids pressing forward to the platform, their hands reaching up to touch his.

The poet announced his first selection, "Execution," a poem about a police chief whom Lermontov accused of killing Pushkin. ("God's judgment is more important than the world's. . . .") The hall immediately hushed. Erect in a light-blue shirt with stiff white collar and cuffs, his blue eyes flashing, Yevtushenko could have been a soldier, part of an honor guard, but as he began to recite in a voice that modulated from crisp announcement to anger to sadness, his right arm, and then his left arm, moving slowly in arcs of emphasis, he was a young Olivier playing Hamlet. A girl on the other side of the stage fainted. There was a flurry of excitement as she was carried out by her friends, the poet in concerned attendance.

He returned, and began his next poem ("My darling, sleep, don't torture me . . ."). It was delivered like a lullaby. The kids began to write notes, fold them, and throw them onto the platform at his feet. These young people were much better looking, more stylish than their elders. Their faces were Eskimo, Russian, Japanese, Indian, everything.

Yevtushenko introduced us to the crowd as his guests. The clapping was loud, and Bill [William Styron] stood to take a bow. They continued to look at us with friendly curiosity, as the poet launched a long new poem, dedicated to an American (see "Doctor Spock," p. 60). Applause, and the photographers, multiple now, jumped up again. A light "Ode to Mushrooms" came next, and then witty stanzas about Russian soldiers who to their delight were taught to read at the end of World War II. ("Masha ate a dictionary for beginners like gruel!") Most poems were delivered completely from memory.

A standing ovation, the traditional rhythmic clapping, and the presentation of flowers and a cap and teal silk robe, which the poet

51

donned onstage, marked the end of the afternoon. Yevtushenko went out the back, squeezing us into a car with him as fans pressed at the doors.*

I Roam Through . . .

I roam through the packed city,
over gay April waters,
I'm revoltingly erratic
and unforgivably young.
I fight my way onto trolleys,
I get carried away in lies,
and I run like mad,
never catching up with myself.
I marvel at the big-hipped barges,
at airplanes
          at my own verses.
I am given a great treasure
and no one explains its purpose.

—1954
TRANSLATED BY HENRY CARLISLE

Mysteries

The mysteries of adolescence fade
like mists dissolved from early shores . . .
Tonyas and Tanyas were mysteries then
though their legs were chapped like ours.

---

*Rose Styron, "Pages from a Tashkent Diary," *Vogue* (September 1, 1969).

52

Stars and animals had secrets, too,
and mushrooms, where the aspens bend,
and doors creaked so mysteriously
only a child could understand.

Conundrums of the universe
popped out like quick bright balls
from an entrancing conjurer's mouth
to entrance us all.

Celestial snowflakes, magic, fell
on glistening fields and groves,
enchanted laughter dazzled
in the eyes of the girls we loved.

Skating, we whispered secret things
on the rink's mysterious ice
and, mystery to mystery, shyly
our fingertips would brush.

Suddenly, we all grew up.
Tailcoat tattered, the conjurer
had gone to tour the far-off land
of another's childhood calendar.

Oh, conjurer, how bad you are,
forgetting us when we're grown!
Upon our shoulders secretless
as snow the snow falls on.

Enchanted spheres, where are you? Even
our sorrows are unmysterious.
Our friends see through us all too well;
we know them by their histories.

And if by chance our hands should touch
gently, in quick caress,
they are only hands, not mysteries
for you and me—alas!

Bring me a mystery, only a mystery—
simple, silent, shy, unknown—
a skinny little barefoot mystery,
only a mystery. One.

—1960
TRANSLATED BY ROSE STYRON

Babi Yar

There are no monuments on Babi Yar,
a steep ravine is all, a rough memorial.
Fear is my ground—
Old as the Jewish people, a Jew myself it seems,
I roam in Egypt in her ancient days,
I perish on the cross, and even now
I bear the red marks of nails.
I am Dreyfus, detested, denounced,
snared behind prison bars:
The petty bourgeousie
is my betrayer and my judge.

54

I am in jail, surrounded,
hounded,
spat upon and slandered.
Shrieking ladies in fine ruffled gowns
brandish their umbrellas in my face.

And now a boy in Bielostok,
I seem to see blood spurt and spread over the floor.
The rowdy ringleaders at the tavern celebrate,
and under the smell of vodka and of onions
and of blood,
kicked by their heavy boots, I lie
begging in vain for pity.
The rampant pogrom roars,
"Kill the Jews—Save Russia!"
A man is beating up my mother.

    O Russian people,
    I know your heart
    lives without boundaries,
    yet men with dirty hands debase you,
    rattling your purest name.
    Shamelessly,
    without the quiver of a nerve
    these pompous anti-Semites call themselves
    "The Union of the Russian People."

Anne Frank, I am she,
a translucent twig of April
and I am filled with love that needs no words.

We are forbidden the sky and the green leaves
but in this dark room we can embrace.
Love, do not fear the noise—it is the rushing
of spring itself.
Come, let us kiss . . .
The sounds of thawing ice change to pounding on the
    door.

Wild grasses rustle over Babi Yar,
the trees stare down, stern as my judge.
Silent the air howls.
I bare my head, graying now,
and I am myself an endless soundless howl
over the buried
thousands and thousands of thousands,
and I am every old man shot down here
and every child.
In no limb of my body can I forget.

Let the Internationale
be sung
when the last reviler of the Jews is dead.
No Jewish blood is mixed in mine, but let me be a Jew
for all anti-Semites to hate, to spit upon.
Only then can I call myself
Russian.

—1961
TRANSLATED BY ROSE STYRON AND OLGA CARLISLE

A Ballad About Nuggets

Night. The town of Fairbanks sleeps,
            exhausted. But invisible
squeakings walk the snowy streets
            cloaked in hides and wool.
Wearing the face of an adolescent
            and a painted caribou parka,
an Eskimo strip-tease *artiste*
            hurries to work in a bar.
Drunken fliers from the air base,
            aching for a shack-up,
ruttish louts, brave buddies,
            throw snowballs at her back.
But she in darkness carries
            her frozen breath
through the leers like a pure
            white rose in her teeth.
In out of the cold
            as hoary as owls,
in through the saloon doors
            come clamorous clouds
with people inside them!—
            a miner, a hunter, a trapper.
They all toss their caps
            on the walrus-tusk hatrack.
Who comes from where?
            What nation? Who cares!
Among these Alaskans
            I'm one of the bears;

for us holy vodka
                    will answer all prayers.
Pal Bob, fellow sourdough, have a drink,
                    down the hatch.
Your big mitts have hugged me,
                    your gray whiskers scratch.
Your grin gleams with gold.
                    You're thin, you look bad, man.
"Listen, Rooshian, I've been prospecting
                    all my life, understand?
No livelier bastard than me swung a pick.
                    Now I'm trash.
My bald head's a runway
                    for mosquitoes and gnats.
Now I'm set to cash in,
                    to add it up proper:
a mouthful of gold
                    and a pocketful of copper.
Ah, when I buried my old lady, Viv,
                    I recall how the sled dogs gave
a howl at the edge of the hole,
                    at the edge of her grave.
Viv was a knockout once, just like
                    those pictures you unfold.
Her body white as quartz all over,
                    with little flecks of gold.
I had a good eye then, as young as you,
                    as lucky and game.
I said to her: 'I've staked you out.
                    Viv, you're my claim.'
I tortured her for forty years.

I was crazy,
Lifelong crazy, to find my strike,
            to find nuggets.
She didn't ask for fancy clothes
            but, shyly,
for a son. She dreamt of a son like me,
            and I, of nuggets.
I drank. Like yellow fish
            alive in a muddy sea,
they came at me, teased me,
            nuggets.
So I closed up shop,
            a bankrupt boss.
My pick and shovel
            made Viv a cross.
I ain't forgot how I dragged that box
            on the hard-froze earth.
I never dug up my nugget,
            I buried her."
Bob counts the coppers in his paw.
            He is drunk, disconsolate.
"Without gold, I . . . 'Scuse me, Rooshian,
            lend me a stake."
Having forgotten his cap,
            he shakily seeks the way out
and jabs the swinging doors
            and plunges into his cloud.
Then I too wander in the dark,
            a child of the saloon.
Nothing pulls on my pockets
            as I walk along.

I still haven't shut up shop,
          I'm too timid;
but perhaps my nugget
          is already buried.
Boyfaced beside me,
          a silent companion,
the Eskimo stripper,
          exhausted, hurries home.
Zero. Icicles
          beard my chin,
and birds frozen in flight fall
          like nuggets, with a clink.

—1967
TRANSLATED BY JOHN UPDIKE

Doctor Spock

I am Doctor Spock, a children's doctor, also
(announced by certain judges, with finality)
a well-known instigator of the country's youth—
a bawler, and a doubtful personality.

Into the frying pan I fling those squabbles
with noxious fillings, and I judge each bout
(Don't let us get annoyed with that man Spock
lest with our diagnosis we carry him out!).

I ask from each of you a better accounting.
Convince us, gentlemen; daringly play your part.
The cardiogram? "All calcified with pain."
X-ray analysis? "Simple stony heart."

60

And they interrogate . . . Okay, interrogate:
"Patient, tell us how you're feeling, pray."
Horrible. "And what is it you complain of?"
Everything. Of everything today.

"The history of your malady?" Well, it is long
and drawn out. I suffer most for all
the children who have seen themselves so strangely,
sunbeams reflected on a shadowed wall.

I loved those funny beings—no teeth, no hair,
their mouths puffy from sucking—oh, they were pips!
The bliss of innocent wisdom on their faces,
our foolish sageness nowhere on their lips. . . .

I saw then, and ever since keep seeing
and comprehending, though I'm no magician,
more in their ageless, changeless "goo" and "da"
than in the artifice of a politician.

In boys brought up in Hell, Hell will abide.
My work has taught me (I keep bulging files)
that he who wants to save a generation
ponders the parents' sin before the child's.

Ah, but the White House is not entirely
a pharmacy! At dark there, people came and saw
witchcraft. Dear people, I mistrust the men who use
your superstitions, and craft them into law. . . .

—1968
TRANSLATED BY ROSE STYRON

ANDREI
VOZNESENSKY

1933—

Andrei Voznesensky, who like his friend Yevtushenko was born in 1933, is extremely popular with poetry lovers around the world. Both poets are nonconformists, both revere the ideals of the Revolution, both are concerned with probing man's consciousness in this paradoxical ever-changing twentieth century. Voznesensky is a first-rate performer: his poetry readings (in which he builds up dramatic communication with his audiences through a slow, intense, resonant voice and the controlled gestures of a body that seems almost awkward in its restraint) have filled stadiums and auditoriums and parks in the Soviet Union and Europe and America for nearly a decade. The places he has visited, actually or in imagination, stud his verses:

> Phosphorescent, Florence glows nightly,
> unlocking every room

63

of her old palazzos. A guardian's key
opens the misty gloom. . . .

from "The Torches of Florence," TRANSLATED BY ROSE STYRON

even when he portrays Gauguin:

To reach the royal Louvre from Montmartre
he did a flip through Java and Sumatra. . . .

from "Parabolic Ballad," TRANSLATED BY ROSE STYRON

or the airports and planes in whose vacuums he professes
to write best:

My self-portrait, neon alembic, apostle of
    heaven's door—
Airport! . . .
Brooklyn Bridge, old fool, grim stone fort;
the monument of this age
is the Airport.

from "The Airport at Night," TRANSLATED BY HENRY CARLISLE

Some day, the poet declares, he will put together a
collection of poems called *Cities Inside Myself*—"New York
Bird," "Paris Without Rhyme," "The Lilac Tree: Moscow-
Warsaw" might be included. "Seek the Indies if you will/
You'll find America!" So ends a book of poems entirely
devoted to his discovery of America, *The Triangular Pear.*
Yet each verse leads us back to the USSR (even California
sequoias suggest Lenin) and that very inward Russian,
Voznesensky himself.

For Voznesensky is quite a different man from Yevtushenko: smaller in stature, more boyish in looks and dress,
quieter in manner and more elusive, less accessible or

64

flamboyant or obviously *engagé*. He was born in Moscow, but spent much of his childhood in the Urals and in the ancient city of Vladimir, coming back to Moscow after the war. His father is a professor of engineering. Both parents have long been interested in art and created a warm cultural atmosphere at home. Voznesensky remembers being profoundly affected by the etchings of Goya that his father carried back from the war—the poet later used Goya as a symbol for war. In Moscow, Andrei studied first painting, then architecture. "Yet all the time," he muses, "poetry was flowing in me like a river under ice." Just as he was about to graduate from the Moscow Architectural Institute it burned to the ground, destroying everyone's work— "model buildings, whole cities!" He took this as an omen, and he abandoned architecture for poetry:

> Fire at the Architectural Institute!
> through all the rooms and over the blueprints
> like an amnesty through the jails . . .
> Fire! Fire!

TRANSLATED BY ROSE STYRON

Voznesensky began to publish in 1958. *Mosaic* came out in 1960. He regarded Pasternak as his master. Though his earliest work may have suggested something of Pasternak's rhythms, he clearly developed an idiom and a viewpoint of his own. His direct style embraced a kind of optimistic lyricism. His most poignant observations were sounded with lightness and tender humor. He was a craftsman of words, etching his lovely seasonal landscapes with images of art, architecture, casual lovers, playful beasts, machines, antimachines. His preoccupation with semantics gradually

65

led to denser textures and charged rhymes; his alert ear brought forth innovative rhythms, new assonances and alliteration, the frequent use of slang and the jargon of the new technologies.

The more praise he received from his audiences, the more criticism was leveled at him officially for his "formalism." Formalism is a term applied to writers who seem to show more concern for form than content—the content, of course, to support Social Realism. When Khrushchev denounced abstract art at the Manège exhibit of 1963, and then bore down on young writers, Voznesensky, just back from France, answered the Premier with irony, promising that now he would "work, work, work." Cautioned to leave Moscow, he wandered for months ("I charge noisily from place to place around Russia. . . .") and, indeed, worked. He wrote love poems and poems of retreat. He composed numerous works that showed the effects of this wounding time on his psyche—"My Achilles Heart," "Give Me Peace," "The Monologue of Marilyn Monroe," "The Ballad of Pain"—and he began the long, complex, prose-and-verse cycle, a love poem to his wife Zoya, "Oza," which presents the poet's views on man's condition in an intriguing, disturbing scientific world. Satire and parody, narrative and hymn, a cyclotron and its toastmasters, a heroine (Oza? Zoya?) who flies through a camouflage of ozone, or melts into thin air—all this leads dramatically to a crazy defense of the human spirit against "the god-damn machine." "To live is marvelous—inexplicable." "To fear technology? That's to go back to the cave!"

The first major poem Voznesensky published on his

return to Moscow and grace was "Longjumeau," a tribute to Lenin. Voznesensky had assured the Party that his loyalty to it would be demonstrated in his work. This did not mean that he would let them dictate his style or language: Lenin is seen playing a kind of skittles, smashing empires and churches and "future Berias"* through the most inventive use of words, meter, and rhyme Voznesensky had yet used.

"Real art," he has said, "is always revolutionary." In the past few years Voznesensky has explored the artist's common battles.

> I love Lorca. I love his name—light as an airborne boat, humming like a theater gallery, sensitive as the moonlike image on a radar screen, with a scent as bitter and pungent as the skin of an orange. . . . He was killed by the Francoists on August 18, 1936. . . . Murderers try to explain this away as "chance." Oh, these "accidents"! Pushkin—a misunderstanding? Lermontov—chance?†
>
> TRANSLATED BY ROSE STYRON AND OLGA CARLISLE

He has concerned himself with the artist's identity ("Who Are We?" "Antiworlds") and his role as prophet ("Master Craftsmen"). Traveling again, Voznesensky endeared himself to gatherings in Europe and America by his gentle perceptions and candid enjoyment of modern life everywhere. His friends are as likely to be scientists as artists. Scientists, he feels, are frequently poetry's most responsive readers. We all "have a great thirst for . . . the symbolic feeling of unity that poetry creates." Since the 1968 politi-

---

*Chief of the secret police under Stalin.

†Federico Garcia Lorca (1899–1936) was a Spanish poet and man of letters. Lermontov, like Pushkin, was killed in a duel; he was twenty-seven.

67

cal crackdown, Voznesensky has guarded his privacy in Russia, publishing poems occasionally in the magazine *Nauka i zhizn'* (*Science and Life*) and *Yunost*. A volume of his collected verse came out in 1970.

Goya

I'm Goya.
A gore-crow pecked out shell craters,
                    my eye sockets, on the naked plain,
                                        unjoyous.

I'm gall

I'm the call
of war, of smoldering towns
                    in the snows of '41.

I'm gaunt

I'm the gorge of the goitred grandma whose hanged
    corpse clanged
                    like a bell on the naked square.

I'm Goya.

O Grapes
of Wrath! In a salvo to the west
I have shot off into outer space
                    the ashes of the uninvited guest

68

and I've tacked hard stars against the commemorative sky

like gauze

I'm Goya.

—1959
TRANSLATED BY JOHN HOLLANDER AND OLGA CARLISLE

The Suburban Train

Boys with trick knives
girls with their teeth crowned
two lady conductors
like sphinxes, drowsing,

the workers doze,
all the coaches nap:
an electric marvel
in the grip of sleep.

But out on the platform
slightly drunken
swaying with the train
odd strings are strumming

and here I linger
at the platform edge
to escape the suffocating
somnolent carriages

69

while pressed around me
like the droning droves
of a gypsy band
are guitars and thieves.

And somehow, oddly,
it comes to pass
that I am reciting
a bit of my verse

to broad-shouldered shadows
to the spit-out husks
of sunflower seeds
and cigarette butts.

Each has a racket of his own
and yet I recite them verse
concerning a little girl who froze
to a windowpane of ice.

They've pled before judges a hundred times
and scarcely blinked at gunfire,
emerging casual and dry
from daily dank adventures.

Then what is the plight of my little girl
or these bouquets of rhyme
to them—to that one, with the ragged curls,
her facepowder thick as loam?

And you there, with the jaded look,
your shirtwaist stamped all over
with fingerprints of half the small-time
swains in Malakhova,

what makes you cry, so unashamed,
and why, in a radiance of tears,
do you come to whisper vulgarly
the purest words in my ear?

Suddenly, off the suburban train
astonishing every eye
truer than Beatrice
you leap, down onto the quay.

—1959
TRANSLATED BY ROSE STYRON

From the Window of a Plane

In the world of friends, where travel is slower,
what do you do there, in the world of rain?
Who shares the segments of your tangerine?
Which exams do you take again?

Or, mistress, full of the charm of arrogance,
do you toss your head, defiant, solemn,
and run like musical hammers out
along the railings, among the columns?

71

O prima donna! do you still play pranks?
Or, chilled because you left your bed
do you wander barefoot, never daring
to lift the receiver's dumbbells of lead?

I hear you've married. Healed, I forget you.
Then why do you freeze as fresh light rain
over the streaming landscape freezes
Freezes

       attentive

              the wing of the plane?

—1960

TRANSLATED BY ROSE STYRON AND OLGA CARLISLE

Autumn in Sigulda

From the last platform of the moving train
    I lean out:
good-by,
good-by, my summer!
    The hour has come.
    The sound of axes echoes outside the summer houses.
    Already the wooden boards have nailed shut my door.
Good-by!

My woods are shorn of their leafy crowns.
Empty and melancholy they stand
    like an old accordion case
    from which the music has gone.

72

We who are men are empty, too,
    and we must go out
    from our sheltering walls,
    from mothers, from girls,
according to old agreements, the eternal order.

Farewell, my mother!
Soon at the window you'll become
    diaphanous as a cocoon
    and when the long afternoon has died, be weary.
Let us sit down together.

Friends and enemies, so long!
    In a moment, hissing like steam
    from inside
you will rush out of me
and I out of you.

Country of my heart, let us say good-by!
    I shall be a star,
    I shall be a willow,
neither do I cry nor plead with you—
thank you, life, for being mine.

Once, in the shooting gallery, with ten shots
    I tried to score a hundred.
    I'm glad I tried.
Glad that into my transparent shoulder blades
    genius has thrust itself
like the ruddy fist of a man into a rubber glove.

73

"Andrei Voznesensky" will live on—
if only it could be
        not just a name or a graven stone
        but pressed against your warming cheek,
"Andrushka."

Do you remember, love, the time you came upon me
in the autumn woods
        and asked me, oh, something,
        dragging by the collar that silly dog
        who wouldn't budge?
My thanks.

I came to life then.
        And for the fall,
        and for explaining me to myself,
for the landlady who got us up at eight
and for the noisy jazz, the hipster songs
        on holidays,
my thanks.

But now you are leaving, leaving
        like a train going out, leaving,
departing through my hollow pores.
We go out of each other as if this house
        were bad for us.

You are still here, yet somehow far away,
        almost in Vladivostok now.

We shall repeat ourselves, I know,
    in friends and lovers,
    in blades of grass—
one, and then another, will replace us.
Nature hates emptiness.

All my thanks, then,
for the wind-shredded crowns of my forest—
    a million leaves
    will come here in our place
and grow, and learn your laws.

But look! There! down the long slope
    a woman runs like a leaf of fire
    behind the train—

Save us!

—1961
TRANSLATED BY ROSE STYRON AND OLGA CARLISLE

Marginalia for Solo Voice
and Tom-Tom: the Negroes Sing

We—
    are Homeric bongos with mirthless eyes, rising
                            like smoke,—
                        we. . .

75

You—
    who are icebox-white, the white of isolation-ward gauze,
                        lifeless zombies—
                you. . .

What, gentlemen, are we singing to all of you about?

About—
your waxy hands, all plastery white, imprinted on those
    sad shoulders of our wives, so weary of being burned
    shamefully—
        ah me!

Yet we
have darkening eyes, though beaten like broken-down
    horses, and cringing for tips in markets and boxing
    rings

Ah—but
when we sleep, or backs at night gleam like starry
    windows.

In us
boxers, gladiators, as in black radiators, or like a pool of
    carp,
constellations are reflected,
    solemn and tender,
        Mars and the Great Bear
                in us . . .

    76

We Negroes, we poets,

                    the planets splash in us

And thus we lie like bags full of stars and myth

Kick us and, punished,
the whole sky reels;
The universe shrieks
Under your heels.

             —1961

             TRANSLATED BY JOHN HOLLANDER AND OLGA CARLISLE

The New York Bird

There on my window sill
sits an aluminum birdie
in arabesques of moonbeam
with a fuselage

             for a body

Above her screw-threaded neck
like a moving flame in place
on a mammoth Zippo lighter,
there shimmers a woman's face!

(Curled up in his capitalist sheets
my friend lies sound asleep)

What? Cybernetic dream?
Ghost and machine at once?
The sauciest dish of all,
or a sort of flying saucer?

   77

Perhaps the American *Geist*
bored with the whole damned show?
Who are you, teen-age monster,
with your held-in-teeth cigarette glowing?

But still in their nightly cold cream
they hand me unblinking affronts,
those eyes—like a girl's up in Michigan
once. . .

She had such wide gas-colored
circles under her eyes—
Oh bird, what can you tell me
—Prophecies, please, not lies.

What surmises? For us, what surprises?
Something peculiar, and from
out there, rises inside me
as if through an intercom

the Atomic Age moans in a bedroom

(I scream. Swearing matricide,
my friend starts up on his mattress
as if he had scalded his hide)

—1961

TRANSLATED BY JOHN HOLLANDER AND OLGA CARLISLE

To Bella Akhmadulina

There are lots of us going. Maybe four of us.
Racing like hell in a car
driven by a girl with bright orange hair . . .
white arms . . . a sporty outfit . . .

Bella, you catastrophic show-off,
you angel from another world!
that beautiful, bratty tilt of your chin . . .
your profile, burning like a white light . . .

The cops in Hell will smack their lips
and send out a special patrol to the gates
when, puffing on a Gauloise, yawning,
you speed past their last law.

Oh, Bella! foot to the floor of the car,
in that voice pure as a church chorale,
you'll say: "Oh, hell! it's so sad—
they've taken my license away!

Did you hear them? they accused me of speeding!
I was only going forty! speeding! . . ."
Oh, Bella, don't worry! the police
know the things of the police,

you know the things of the sky, the sounds
of the light-years. During these light-years
let's disappear, let's go, throwing off rays!
It may be that no one will be bringing home prizes.

79

Slam down the gas pedal, Bella, heavenly hawk!
Let's scatter our bones if we have to . . .
Long live your singing speed,
the deadliest of speeds!

What patterns, what white lines lie ahead of us?
There are only a few of us going. Maybe four.
Racing like hell . . . and you are a goddess!
And we are a majority after all.

—1964

TRANSLATED BY JEAN VALENTINE AND OLGA CARLISLE

Mihail Svetlov

Yevgeny Vinokurov

Alexander Mezhirov

THE WAR
GENERATION

The writers presented in this chapter were born in the first quarter of this century. They have one thing in common: they are dedicated poets using restrained voices and well-established literary forms. They follow in the traditions of Russian poetry, before it was overtaken by the heroic voices celebrating the October Revolution. Of these voices, Mayakovsky's was the loudest and the clearest:

> Ringed
>> by rifle
>>> and cannon barking
> Moscow's
>> an island
>>> where we stand,
> We—the beggars,
>> we—the starving.
> Heads full of Lenin
>> and gun in hand.

FACING PAGE: *Naum Korzhavin (above left), Boris Slutzky (above right), Daniel Andreyev with his wife on his return from prison*

THIS PAGE: *Vadim Andreyev (upper left), Boris Poplavsky (upper right), Nicholas Zabolotzky*

But many other poets—not necessarily imitators of Mayakovsky—sang of gallant revolutionary deeds. For example, Mihail Svetlov (1903–1964) is best remembered for his "Granada" (1926). Describing a Russian civil war episode, "Granada" illustrates the mood of feverish violence which swept through Russia during the first years of the Soviet era:

> I went off to fight
> with a gun and a pack
> so the poor in Granada
> could get their land back.
>
> Farewell to my village.
> Farewell to my home.
> Granada, Granada,
> Granada my own!
>
> We yearned as we galloped
> to master at once
> the grammar of battle,
> the language of guns.
> The sun rose above us,
> descended again;
> Our horses grew weary
> of pounding the plain.
>
> "The Song of the Apple"*
> adapted its rhymes

---

*A well-known ballad of the Russian civil war period.

to the rhythm of riding,
the woe of the times.
And where is your song, pal?
Listen—a moan?
Granada, Granada,
Granada my own. . . .

Our squad hardly noticed
the loss of a man.
"The Song of the Apple"
at daybreak began.
But softly at nightfall
the Russian rain
mourned the Ukrainian
fallen for Spain.

TRANSLATED BY MARGARET WITTLIN

In 1971 these heroic voices are still echoing across the USSR. However, almost imperceptibly, their impact is fading away. Mayakovsky is no longer Russia's most popular poet. In Russian letters one detects a new search for roots, a return to traditions both in terms of meter and of sensibility. Today's Soviet poets are often more interested in such old-fashioned topics as Love and Nature than in tales of revolutionary prowess. This is as true of their readers. A whole group of talented poets are also intent on telling Russians about the reality of warfare rather than about Bolshevik lore. The younger ones remind us of American writers like Norman Mailer and Joseph Heller, Karl Shapiro and Robert Lowell, who are their contemporaries. The novelist Alexander Solzhenitsyn belongs to this generation, which both in America and in the USSR is notable for its strong antimilitaristic convictions. They are the poets who fought in World War II as young men and who thus share a sense of identity. They all use conventional forms, possibly because anything resembling modernism was forbidden in the Soviet Union during their formative years.

Yevgeny Vinokurov, Alexander Mezhirov, Naum Korzhavin, and Boris Slutzky are anthologized here. Among their peers are Vladimir Kornilov, Nicholas Panchenko, Yuri Levitansky, David Samoylov, and Victor Sokolov—and, of course, the versatile Bulat Okudzhava, who besides poetry has composed many immensely popular subtle songs which he sings to his own guitar accompaniment. Okudzhava has also written two works of fiction: *Lots of Luck, Kid!* (1960) and the remarkable *Poor Avrosimov* (1969).

Yevgeny Vinokurov (1925—), a younger member of the "war generation," celebrates Spring in a sensitive if somehow unexceptional manner:

> Place midnight in the care of my hands
> where fresh wet lilacs rustle;
> its delicate petals I'll not distress
> but accent, soft, its sounds.

> Give me the lightning of May, dense rain,
> far dawns and secret woodland:
> no leaf shall I crumple nor frail grass bend,
> but rhyme the birch trees' murmuring.

Lend me a river's pool, brimming with sky,
sharp star-fins and steep-sloped shore;
no twilight fields will I trample, but gently
drop commas here and there.

TRANSLATED BY ROSE STYRON AND OLGA CARLISLE

Alexander Mezhirov (1923—   ) is in love with Georgia
in the Caucasus. This is a country which has been a source
of inspiration for Russian poets since Pushkin and
Lermontov. Mezhirov has done many distinguished translations from the Georgian, following in the footsteps of
Boris Pasternak, who was a brilliant translator from that
tongue. Mezhirov has used Georgian subject matter in his
own verse:

A funeral in Tchiatura, in the mountains, mine:
like black soot I was falling lightly on the road.

Everlasting mourning. Leaves and grass are
    blue-black in Tchiatura.
A miner's ore-filled gondola, my coffin, was carried out.

There was crying in the house, and on the black meadow
    a drunken feast, a wake. Pagan and Christian

revelers were all the same. Do you remember lightning
striking that black poplar? Fire burned it to its roots

and buried itself deep in the black earth of the pass.
I said, "I'll find that mountain pass, and, remembering
    the storm,

89

dig up the lightning, bring it as a gift for you."
Instead, I found my grave.

The house is shaken with sobs, the meadow filled with
drunken wailing.
—Or is it evil insomnia, a black light rushing

at my window space, to blaze, enter,
stand at my bed? Insomnia will murder me.

The noise of a motor being clumsily cranked under the
window
makes my head throb. I cannot sleep. Tortured

is the calm of night. Stop that senseless sputtering
noise!
Stop cranking it! Dry out the points!

Toward dawn, the end, I will fall asleep and dream
that in a black grave in Tchiatura, over the sounds

of song and lamentation I am buried, next to a flash
of lightning black as my dream.

TRANSLATED BY ROSE STYRON AND OLGA CARLISLE

Naum Korzhavin (1923—   ) sings of the girls of his
native Kiev, touching on a theme which is recurrent in
modern Soviet literature—a sense of concern in the face
of all that Russian women have had to bear in the last fifty
years because of wars and persecutions. Here is his

For the Girls in My Home Town:

In Kiev again! Fair girls with their tender sauntering
are all like you, but you I'll meet no more in this town.
Girls from before the war, my childhood, sweet girls of
  Kiev,
my grown-up friends, what is your way now? Where
  have you gone?

When I was young I never dared to kiss your feet
nor to explain what I still tried to know myself.
I left you alone in childhood, as in my memory
and let you fall away, cutting off a limb of my life.

Sometimes we met, and talked, but I had no time—
I was breaking a path with my shoulder, forging my way
and then that false age stabbed me, lifted me from you
as if you'd had no part in the pain of that day.

As if it weren't you, and your unfulfilled romances,
your weddings, divorces, gusts of anxiety, lostness . . .
The loves that you dreamed never found their own
  image
and somehow you could not settle for any love less.

I knew, but I wasn't thinking of you: I was playing
roles, hating all southern ways, primed not to listen.
This nonsense made me forget that pain is pain
in any guise, true of our every destiny.

91

There's nothing to do. We live, have our affairs.
We manage; even if things go wrong, it's life, not a
    calvary.
The past can't redeem its unkept promise of happiness,
nor love be reaped that was sown at an outworn
    ceremony.

These girls with their tender saunter are you no longer,
who hurried by full of trust, as they hurry now.
I look for you everywhere—I'm like you, from Kiev!
The same southern blood, chilled by the winds of
    Moscow.

I'm you! And my sense of guilt is quite complete,
my course now seems a bankruptcy self-wrought,
as if I could have loved and taken you all
away, and saved your dreams, and stupidly have not.

TRANSLATED BY ROSE STYRON

These next lines, which are something of a motto for
a number of poets of his age—those who have suffered
most from Stalinist repressions and from the political
inertia which these repressions induced—are also his:

We may gather rhymes, long or short
as much as we like—
No one will summon us to the Senate Square,
nor in heavy carriages through the snow
will true women follow us now.

TRANSLATED BY OLGA CARLISLE

This is an evocation of the wives of the Decembrists who
went into Siberian exile with their husbands, after an

92

abortive *coup d'état* against the czar. (The Decembrists were a group of aristocrats who challenged czarist autocracy and attempted a rebellion on the Senate Square in St. Petersburg on December 14, 1825.)

Boris Slutzky (1919—   ) explores the fate of the poet in modern society in weighty, almost prosaic lines. "Poets and Physicists" is a great favorite of Moscow students:

Nowadays physicists are honored
and poets are not.
It is not a matter
of dry numbers.
It is rather
a universal law.

Somehow we must have failed;
the wings of Pegasus were weak,
and our verses insipid.
We did not soar.
Nowadays physicists are honored,
and poets are not.

This is quite obvious.
Why argue, or be hurt?
Instead
let us look
at how our rhymes
evaporate like foam

while, sedately,
greatness
retreats into logarithms.

TRANSLATED BY OLGA CARLISLE

Older members of the war generation, Daniel Andreyev (1906–1958) and Vadim Andreyev (1903—   ) were the sons of the Russian playwright Leonid Andreyev by his first marriage. The two brothers were spiritually very close but they lived separated most of their lives. Daniel was a Muscovite; as for Vadim, he was forced to emigrate to France during the Revolution, when he was sixteen. Daniel, brought up in the sunny environment of his mother's family, developed into a poet of great originality. He was profoundly religious—visionary at times both in his verse and in his extensive philosophical writings. Though a small Soviet elite holds him in high esteem, only very few of his works have yet been published in the USSR: Daniel Andreyev was hostile to Stalin's dictatorship. Arrested in 1947 for writing a subversive novel, he spent ten years in a special prison in the medieval town of Vladimir near Moscow. He emerged from prison after the death of Stalin a broken man physically. Yet he was still able to live out two years, savoring the promise of freedom heralded by the Khrushchev era and a brief reunion with his brother. He had fought heroically in World War II: here is his vision of the siege of Leningrad (1941–1943), in which more than three million Russians reportedly died of starvation. The Russian troops are at last breaking into the dying city (this is a free adaptation of part of his epic-length "The Russian Gods"):

94

Night winds! Dark mountainous skies
over the snowy bier of Leningrad!
You are our trial and our great reward
and I keep, treasured as a medal won
the memory of that evening: on the black ice
path, I mixed my stubborn
steps with others of the Russian race—
somber, covered in steel to its eyes.

From Moscow's hills, from Saratov's meadows
where waves of rye vibrate in summer,
from taiga's heartland where centenary cedars
give birth to a deep
howling, for a bitter military deed
the law drove as one our races.
From drifts of snow to floating glaciers
we stretched like a long live rope.

We were lawyers and farmers, accountants,
   woodsmen,
the nasty dogs from the people's kennels,
young boys with turned-up noses, criminals
and old men charged with vigor.
Scythed by a giant were the plains of Peter—
six-meter tree stumps like stalks in the air—
the snow smelled of smoke, of old battles
where Russia reared, and plunged in a fiery ocean.

Hunger, like entrails, twisted within us
and yeastily rose, disturbing our heads

and each of us sensed that in those gray paws
all faith and reason yields.
It welded our eyes shut, it coated our souls
with ice: all we could think of was eating—
that mean-browed spirit, Hunger, breeding
sorrow formless as death.

Our march was beginning across Lake Ladoga.
Darkness deepened. Off to the south
in angry arcs the flares of the Germans
would intermittently rise.
The wind grew stronger, determined to drown
in blackness their supernatural rainbows
cloaking their hostile zodiac
in a heavy funeral shroud. . . .

But night was hunting us, haunting
the gates of the lost city. Denser and denser
the frosts of January climbed like smoke
from the Finnish side. It was a desert.
Only the anguished souls of old buildings,
their ancient stones, a lingering wall
were lifted still,
spattering the sky with clots of India ink.

TRANSLATED BY ROSE STYRON AND OLGA CARLISLE

Vadim Andreyev, on the other hand, witnessed World
War II in Western Europe. He was active in the French
Resistance against the Germans. "Rebecca" is typical of this
thoughtful poet whose sensibility remained totally Russian
despite his many years in exile:

Before her mirror Rebecca combs out her dark
   hair.
The Biblical promise shall not come true.
Over the empty road the yellowing dust
like a transparent rose will stand and stand.

The sunset fades. The rose is withering.
A song in the dark is foreshadowing tears.
You'll extend the palm of your hand to the sky,
and a handful of darkness will bloom. . .

Your hair is cut off. On the dirty floor,
brown and alive, your braids are lying.
Your frightened eyes, two pale-blue wasps,
avidly search the unspeakable sight.

The Prophet's prediction shall not come true.
Cassandra alone knew what would come.
For life was only the dry yellow sand,
the sifting sand of childhood games.

And because Rebecca will never return,
we do not dare raise our eyes to the sky
—This burning sunset, this empty sky,
this weighty world which is choking us.

TRANSLATED BY OLGA CARLISLE

Another *émigré* poet was Boris Poplavsky (1903–1935),
a member of the Russian Bohemia which flourished around
Montparnasse in Paris before World War II. In those years
the Parisian–Russian colony nurtured the painters Soutine

and Chagall, the novelist Nabokov, the composer Stravinsky, and many other artists of international accomplishment. Out of a number of poets who formed the Paris school of Russian poetry (this group included Ivan Bunin, Vladislav Khodasevich, Marina Tsvetayeva, Georgi Ivanov, Anna Prismanova, Alexander Ginger, Boris Bozhnev, and others), Poplavsky alone was directly influenced by the French poetic styles of the times, notably by surrealism. Yet a Slavic nostalgia permeates his verse; a dream of pre-Revolutionary Russia is superimposed on the Paris of the thirties, as in "Flags":

> On a summer day above the sidewalks
> paper lanterns were suspended.
> A trumpet's voice rasped. Over the avenue
> flags dreamt on their long poles.
>
> A wave of heat and they were trembling,
> the sea was somewhere near.
> The air was dreamless like Lethe.
> We wept with sorrow for the flags. . . .

TRANSLATED BY OLGA CARLISLE

A brilliant man with a vast, somehow esoteric erudition, Poplavsky died accidentally while he and a friend were experimenting with drugs. He died young but he had been able to express something of the mood which affects us today in the age of Aquarius. Here is his "Pitying Europe," written in 1930 and dedicated to the eminent Russian critic Mark Slonim:

Europe, O Europe in youthful mourning,
how slowly your flags unfurl in moonlight!
Legless people are laughing at war. From the park
a rocket is launched to the moon.

Skyscrapers have raised their multicolor banners.
Was the launching successful? At sea, far away,
the endless days of summer are stretching,
and a ship is departing in a line of gray . . .

Europe, O Europe, your parks are teeming!
In a white taxi, Ophelia is reading a paper,
while smiling Hamlet dreams his dreams of
    freedom.
He is crushed by the wheels of a tram.

Far away, gasworks are burning.
A huge sun is setting in the yellow sea.
Europe, O Europe, your ship is sinking!
In the dance hall trumpets are playing prayers.

People remembered trams, trees and autumn
as they slowly went down. In their evening
    clothes,
the laughing Europeans went down into the
    ocean
asking each other: "Are you frightened?" "No."

The sunsets glowed again over the city towers,
where lovers were singing of immortal spring.
They wept in the mornings, choking with pity
when they chanced to see the past in their dreams.

On the empty avenues, the rain, exhausted,
settled at the fences like an autumn fever.
We too were dying, having waited vainly
—sickly workmen in a high-rise building.

TRANSLATED BY OLGA CARLISLE

Within the Soviet Union a more classic note was struck
by Nicholas Zabolotzky (1903–1958)—although he too
wrote surrealistic poems in his youth. He was the son of
an agronomist and, like Sergei Yesenin, sprang from a
Russian village. A man of great gentleness and integrity,
he was arrested in 1937, in the Great Purges, and spent
years in concentration camps of the Altai region in the Far
East. He returned to Moscow in 1946 and was able to
resume his literary career. His late works unite solemnity
of style with a haunting sense of nature, typical of many
nineteenth-century Russian writers. Zabolotzky's contemporaries—all poets of accomplishment—are Vladimir
Lugovsky, Leonid Martynov, Olga Bergholts, Simon
Kirsanov, Victor Bokov, Yaroslav Smelyakov, and Alexander Tvardovsky, the author of a popular World War II
epic, *Vasily Tyorkin,* and once the distinguished editor of
the best Soviet magazine, *Novii mir.* None of these writers,
however, quite have Zabolotzky's poetic conviction.

When the Light of Day Fades

In black night, after the sun has set,
the sky folds over the huts, changing,
glittering like the particles of a huge atom
webbed together in an invisible net—

100

And I know that in the dark, somewhere
in another part of the world in a garden
like this one, the same night, the same stars
shine through the immortal black air.

In that garden, another poet, alone,
stares at the night sky and wonders
why an aged, distant man torments him
with vague thoughts, night images in their dark tone.

TRANSLATED BY JAMES SCHEVILL AND OLGA CARLISLE

The Fireflies

Words glow like lanterns of the fireflies;
Turn away, as distractedly, I see them wink out,
their virgin flames invisible in the dark
where their corpses live for all to doubt.

But if you look at them in a Black Sea spring
while oleanders sleep at dusk in solemn blooms,
the fireflies shine, spindrift, into the night
and waves fall on the shore, in endless dooms . . .

As they die, the fireflies fix the world
in one breath as the earth spins;
forgetting the meaning of Creation, the firefly words
in the summer storms are but flickering pins.

101

The echo of thunder and lightning-flash
are playing their fanfare over the sea.
What are poor words? They tick like insects
yet fly to my hand and sometimes obey me.

TRANSLATED BY JAMES SCHEVILL AND OLGA CARLISLE

The Juniper Tree

In my dream I saw the wind blow
through the distant, metallic branches
of a juniper tree; the amethyst berries
rang like affectionate bells through my sleep
and the pleasant smell of resin
hovered in the soft air.
Sleepwalker, I moved around the trunk
and saw caught in the low, dark branches
the faint image of your smile.
Juniper tree, juniper tree,
your light wind-song, scented with resin,
pierced me with quick needles of death
as the cool murmur of her changeable lips
faded in the wakening air.
Beyond my window, clouds float
through a golden sky.
I stare at my lifeless, empty garden.
God forgive you, juniper tree.

TRANSLATED BY JAMES SCHEVILL AND OLGA CARLISLE

102

SERGEI YESENIN

1895–1925

The life of Sergei Yesenin was not a long one but his pen was ready early and he was endowed with an exceptional lyric gift. Born in 1895, Yesenin as a boy was a shepherd among the peasants of Ryazan province. He studied to be a teacher. Then, captivated by his reading of the peasant poet Nikolai Kluyev, and of the symbolist Alexander Blok, he turned to composing poetry. Its melody and sensuous imagery evoked the soft beauty of rural Russia—in St. Petersburg at twenty, so did he. Yesenin was handsome. When called upon to recite his verses, he would take the platform wearing a peasant blouse sashed in colorful silk, and all but sing them. Folklore seemed reality; village saints and a country Virgin moved vividly through the landscape for his rapt audiences.

Day of the Dead, his first book, was hailed in 1916 Moscow. Yesenin quickly became enamored not only of the literary life but of the Revolution, supporting first the socialist revolutionaries, then the Bolsheviks, convinced

105

that they would lead Russia to a Promised Land of the Spirit. The two volumes he published next (*Otherland*, 1918, and *Transfiguration*, 1919) demonstrated his faith that, armed with a kind of mystical Christianity, the rebels would transform Russia into a democratic peasant-principled utopia. Yesenin moved to Moscow. Carefree and dashing, he was a popular figure there. He easily took on the leadership of a new group of poets, the Imaginists, who put memorable images above all other requirements for poetry.

The grim realities of the Russian civil war, the bleakness of industrialization, brought disenchantment to the poet. The countryside he idealized was invaded by progress. He tried to make his writing and his life fit the times. A new hero of his verse was Pugachev, a Cossack who led a peasant rebellion during Catherine the Great's reign. A new pastime was drinking, and he explored taverns nightly in the lowest company he could find. His extravagant ways, his succession of international escapades on trips to France, Germany, and the United States, his love affairs and quarrels and broken marriages—especially the one to the American dancer Isadora Duncan—soon were as renowned as his poems. *Moscow of the Taverns* and *Confessions of a Hooligan*, 1923 and 1924, were his published attempts at toughness. But more and more, in his best verse, he lamented the disappearance of his pastoral "wooden Russia."

Nostalgia, tragedy, echoed. In a poem called "Letter to My Mother," he assures her that he will not drink himself to death before coming to see her again:

I love you as before, and now my only dream
is to leave this restless torment, to start again
   for home.
When our white garden boughs spread with
   blossoms I'll return,
   only this time you must let me sleep through dawn.

In 1924 Yesenin did try to return home. After a last trip abroad, unable to come to terms with the Soviet world, he traveled for the first time in eight years to his native village, Konstantinov. But he and it had changed so much they barely recognized each other. At Christmas time, after composing "Soviet Russia," the poetic account of his visit home, he went to St. Petersburg. There, alone in a hotel on December 27, 1925, he slit his wrists, wrote a suicide note in his own blood, and hanged himself.

His alienation had been complete. Yet his works continued to be read and praised, his death pondered. Mayakovsky, in his poem "Letter to Yesenin," written in 1926, upbraids him for civic irresponsibility ("In this life it isn't hard to die—/The challenge is to make life new.") Later, Mayakovsky took his own life. In his autobiography Pasternak writes of them both:

> In the poet who imagines himself the measure of life and pays for it with his life, the Romantic conception manifests itself brilliantly and irrefutably. . . . In this sense something inscrutable was incarnate both in the life of Mayakovsky and in the fate of Yesenin, which defies all epithets, demanding self-destruction and passing into myth.*

And in the younger generation, Yevtushenko, the metropolitan poet whose peasant roots are deeply nurtured cries:

---

*Boris Pasternak, *Safe Conduct* (New York: New Directions, 1958), p. 116.

Yesenin, give me for luck your tenderness
to meadows and birches, to beast and man. . . .

Then, in another "Letter to Yesenin," which deplores the
current literary policies of the Komsomol (the communist
youth organization) and the squabbles in "Parnassus," he
declares that each poet is part-Yesenin:

And I am Yesenin, though different, of course.
In a kholkhoz since birth was my rosy horse.
I, like Russia, have grown steely,
and Russian, there is less birch in me.

My dear Yesenin, how Russia's changed!
It's silly to weep, and there may be danger. . . .

Life chokes us, caught in the wheel of a car
as her scarf choked Isadora.

But we must live . . . there's no salvation
in vodka, suicide, or women.
It's Russia that must save us now,
and your sincerity, Yesenin.

TRANSLATED BY ROSE STYRON

O Fields . . .

O fields, fields, ploughed fields
the sadness of Kolomna
is on my heart like yesterday—
inside it, Russia shines.

108

Now beneath my horses' hoofs
like birds the long miles sing
and over me in handfuls
the sun sprinkles its rain.

O land of terrored floods
and the gentle ways of spring,
all that I know I've learned from you,
learned from your stars and dawn.

And I meditated and read
from the Bible of the winds
and thereupon my golden cows
Isaiah helped me tend.

—1917
TRANSLATED BY ROSE STYRON

Prayers for the First Forty Days

of the Dead (a fragment)

Have you seen the locomotive
on its cast-iron hoofs
charge across the countryside
dodging in and out of mists
hissing by the lake through its nostrils of iron?

And running awkwardly beside—
as in some desperate race
on an overgrown gymkhana course—

109

springing through the high grass,
its slender legs flung out too far, a foal with a red
   mane?

Dear, foolish little colt!
Where, why does he race?
Hasn't he heard that cavalries
of steel have conquered live steeds
and all his chasing, galloping, over the sad plain

cannot catch those days gone by
when Pechenegs would barter
a pair of lovely Russian girls
of the steppes for a single horse?
Fate in the marketplace has changed.

The color of our deep and tranquil
waters has awakened them
to the noise of gnashing steel,
the braying train,
and spent, for a locomotive, tons of horseflesh and skin.

—1920
TRANSLATED BY ROSE STYRON

Soviet Russia

Here where the hurricane raged by
   how few of us remain.
The lattice of old friendships
   shows pieces missing now.

To my lately orphaned birthplace I
   guide myself again.
Though eight years of footsteps
   hurried the other way.

And who can I cry out to?
   Who'll walk with me, to share
the melancholy joy I feel
   finding I'm still alive?
Even the wooden bird I knew
   when I was a child is here,
its eyes shut: the windmill
   with one wing left to wave. . . .

"Already you've begun to fade
   to wither like a flower
and other young men all too soon
   are singing other
songs, and surely they will sound
   more interesting by far
for not this town alone
   but all earth is their mother."

Oh, my country, what an absurdity
   I see that I've become!
My hollow cheeks with dry color
   blushing, like a clown's!
All at once alien to me
   is the language of my countrymen
and I am a foreigner
   in my own town. . . .

—1924

TRANSLATED BY ROSE STYRON AND OLGA CARLISLE

Suicide Note

Good-by, my friend,
dear friend, good-by!
Stay in my heart.
This separation
planned for us by destiny
foretells a far reunion.

No hand, no word,
my friend, good-by!
No tears or look
of grieving.
Death is not novel in this life.
There's little new in living.

—1925
TRANSLATED BY ROSE STYRON

Mayakovsky as a student in the School of Painting, 1911–1912

VLADIMIR MAYAKOVSKY

1893–1930

*A*re involvement in politics and the reform of society more important for an artist than the pure pursuit of his art? It is an old and a perpetually new question, and the biography of the poet Vladimir Mayakovsky should be of special interest to all who ask it.

Born in 1893, the son of a forest ranger in Transcaucasia, Mayakovsky belonged to the impoverished gentry. He hated school, he hated the mountains and longed for the cities. When his father died, he moved to Moscow and immediately, at fifteen, began working for the Bolshevik underground. So did his sisters, Lyuda and Olya. He was soon arrested; he spent a year in prison and there began to write poetry. He had already been studying painting. After his release he became increasingly involved in poetry and joined the bohemian, publicity-seeking, often-brilliant Futurists, a group of diverse artists who celebrated the Revolution and the new beauty of an industrialized Russia. He gained instant fame at eighteen as he wrote and acted

115

in Futurist films, fashioned anticapitalist cartoons and posters, and traveled all over Russia, making speeches, wearing a bright yellow tunic and in his lapel a wooden spoon. He propelled himself—tall, robust, handsome—as the poet-spokesman of the working class.

> The enemy of the working class masses
> is my enemy, too, sworn and long-standing.
> Years of toil and days of hunger
> ordered us under the red flag.

Mayakovsky was an "engaged poet." He was in love with revolution, with everything gigantic and modern. His poems are a crescendo of sweeping abstractions and over-sized metaphors. He created a new, appropriately coarse texture for his poetry, a language of colloquialism, puns, and rough images which have been imitated ever since. His poem "Atlantic Ocean" is a good example of his approach to nature—it is built on images of guerrilla warfare!

Not a party member himself, Mayakovsky worked tirelessly for the Communists as a propagandist and educator, believing that communism alone could bring social justice and happiness to his country. He was delighted by his fame, his ability to travel freely in Europe and America. He was dazzled by Paris. But little by little, as the Communist party became more autocratic under Stalin's leadership, the acknowledged "Poet of the Revolution" was trapped in an official role, that of a servant of the state. Critics began to hound him. Stalin was promoting an atmosphere of political intimidation and suspicion, encouraging writers to denounce each other's "petit-bourgeois leanings." Although Mayakovsky could scarcely believe it, he too was accused of being a corrupt bourgeois writer. He was denied a passport to join his fiancée, a young *émigrée* living in Paris. He wrote a last autobiographical poem, "In Full Voice," and then, on April 14, 1930, profoundly depressed, he shot himself in his studio in Moscow.

Two contemporaries of Mayakovsky recorded their last sight of him. The poet Olga Bergholts:

> I will never forget how, in the Press House, at Vladimir Mayakovsky's "Twenty Years' Work" exhibition, almost boycotted for some reason by "adult" writers, we—a handful of people from the young writers' group "Relay"—were on duty literally for days by the stands, physically suffering at the sight of the tall man: with a sad and austere face, arms folded behind him, he paced the empty rooms, as if waiting for someone very dear to him and becoming more and more convinced that this person would not come. We did not dare approach him, and only Boris [the poet Boris Kornilov] audaciously suggested a billiards game to him. Vladimir Vladimirovich willingly accepted the proposition and we all felt better somehow; of course, we all went into the billiards room to look at "our Kornilov playing with Mayakovsky". . . .*

and the critic Victor Shklovsky:

> I saw him for the last time in the Writers' House on Vorovsky Street. The room was lit by spotlights placed in the corners in such a way that the light got in one's eyes.
> A man passed, then another. They carried briefcases. They were on their way to talk about organization matters. A short man passed, bald, his skull covered with pale skin.
> He was carrying a large, shiny case.
> He was in great hurry: he was going to re-educate Mayakovsky.
> Vladimir went by, stopped for a while.
> He talked.

*Wiktor Woroszylski, *The Life of Mayakovsky* (New York: The Orion Press, 1970), p. 590.

117

He began to praise the living communes, which he formerly had not trusted.

They must have convinced him, obviously.*

Stalin chose to ignore the protest implicit in Mayakovsky's suicide. At his instigation, the poet was all but canonized in Russia: heroic portraits were commissioned, a huge bronze statue erected on Gorky Street in Moscow. Reactions to his death differed greatly, due to world politics and to the poet's own personality. The French Leftists mourned him, but certain Russian literary émigrés, like the writers Nabokov and Bunin, declared that he had never been first-rate. Despite these controversies, Mayakovsky survives today as a true poet, his rhythms, his brutal words, and original style still contemporary and effective.

Atlantic Ocean

Spanish stone eyes hurting
and white walls like a saw's tooth—
the ship ate coal, drank fresh water
until twelve o'clock.
At one o'clock the ship grunted,
chewed at its muzzle, breathed heavily—
off at full speed.
Europe grew smaller. Europe took off.
The water tons of it like years
ran by us, above the birds,
below fish,
everywhere water.

---

*Ibid., p. 513.

For weeks
the ocean works hard, then gets
drunk. Today it sighed,
shouted up from a broad chest,
"How I'd like to get my ass on the Sahara.
Spit, man. There's a ship near, let's sink her,
or throw her off center
with our wave curl.
If she comes out dry
I'll make fish soup out of her.
But who wants small-fry people?
All right, Let 'em hug their insides
and sail on."
Waves are teasers, their splashes
can bring up a man's childhood,
for somebody else a sweetheart's voice.
Well as for me,
they make me want to run up a flag!
Bang! Crash! Afterwards
clear water and nobody's afraid. Just then
a member of the Revolutionary
Committee, a giant wave,
gets up on his haunches from the depths.
And a guard of drops, water partisans,
flies to the sky
and falls down,
tearing to shreds
the imperial robe of foam.
And again the waters unite
and command the wave to surge,
a leader.

119

The huge wave crashes down.
It rains slogans
and orders.
The waves are not going to give up,
(as they swear to the Central Water Committee)
short of victory.
They throw everything into it—
and they win! Unlimited Soviet power
riding the final spume—
there go the water drops around the world—
circling the equator . . .
Now a time for small Committee meetings,
serious talk in the subdued foam.
Ocean, scrubbed, clean, smiling,
brought to heel. I'm calm, also.
I lean over the rail. Good luck, Comrades!
I see you're still at it, under the ship's ladder,
you local committee executives,
are sweating away. Below
in a neat, efficient manner
a coral palace is being built,
improved housing for a worker whale family.
For dedicated him and her and nursery whale.
Someone's even thought of the moon
and laid it down like a forest path,
you might crawl over it on your belly.
Spy-eye Atlantic is watching out
for the enemy. That one's not going
to get an easy slick ride. Now it is
cold on the moon-lighted water; now
you lie moaning, drenched in the foam

of your wounds. I look, I am looking.
Sea, you are my relative, loved and next
to my heart. In my ear remains forever
the noise of that battle.
I wish I could empty you into my eyes.
Your bigness, your spirit, your work,
your blood—
revolutionary ocean you are my elder brother.

—1925
TRANSLATED BY BARBARA GUEST

In Full Voice (First Introduction)

Most respected comrade descendants!
Excavating in this day's petrified crap,
probing the darkness of our century,
you might, possibly, ask about me too.
And, possibly, your scholars will tell you,
smothering problems in their learned terms,
that once there lived a bard of boiled water,
and dedicated enemy of unboiled water.
Professor, remove those bicycle specs!
I'll tell you myself
                    about my times
                              and me.
I, the sewer cleaner and waterboy,
drafted and mobilized by the Revolution
went off to the front from the baronial gardens
of poetry—capricious broad.

121

She planted a pretty garden,
kids,
        cottage,
                pond,
                        and lawn.
"Myself a garden I did sow
and watered it to make it grow."
Some pour poems from watering cans,
others spit water from their mouths—
curlyheaded Mitreky,
                        clever-minded Kudreky—
but what in hell is it all about!
There's no end to them—
beneath the walls they mandolin:
"Tara-tina, tara-tina,
twang . . ."
It's no great honor that among such roses
my sculpture soars
over public squares where TB wheezes,
and whores stroll with their spivs and syphilis.

Agitprop* sticks in my craw too,
I'd rather spin love songs for you—
There's more profit in it,
                        it's more attractive.
But I have mastered myself,
standing on the throat
                        of my own song.
Listen, comrade descendants,
to the agitator, the rabble-rouser.

*Propaganda and agitation in behalf of communism.

122

Silencing torrents of poetry,
I'll skip the slim volumes;
alive, I'll speak to the living.
I'll come to you in the Communist hereafter
and not like a singsong Yesenin messiah.
My verse will reach you

across sierras of time,
over heads of poets and governments.
My verse will reach you, but not
like an arrow in a lyrical cupid hunt,
not as an old penny

reaches the coin man,
not as a dead star's light reaches you.
My verse by labor will break through the years
and appear,

ponderous,

crude,

plain,
as an aqueduct built by slaves
of Rome enters our days.
When, in mounds of books,

where verse lies interred,
you discover the iron fragments of lines,
handle them with respect
like old but menacing weapons.
It is not my habit

to caress

the ear

with words;
the maiden's ear, ringed with curls,
will never blush from my innuendoes.

Deploying on parade the armies of my pages,
I shall review the lines.
The verses stand heavy as lead,
ready for death and immortal fame.
The poems are rigid,

                  their gaping titles
aimed muzzle to muzzle.
The cavalry of witticisms aligned
to launch a shouting charge, stands steady,
leveling the pointed lances of its rhymes.
And all these troops armed to the teeth,
which have passed in victory

                  for twenty years,
all these, to the very last page,
I present to you,

             proletarian of this planet.
The enemy of the working-class masses
is my enemy too, sworn and long-standing.
Years of toil and days of hunger
ordered us under the red flag.
We opened each volume of Marx
as we would open the shutters of our own house,
but even without reading we could decide
which side to join, which side to fight on.
Our dialectics were not learned from Hegel.
In the clang of battle,

             they burst forth in verse
when,

     under fire,

         the bourgeois turned back,

124

as we once
        turned back from them.
Let fame follow genius
as an inconsolable widow
            follows the hearse—
and so die, my verses,
                die like common soldiers,
die as our men died, nameless in attack.
I spit
        on the tons of bronze.
I spit
        on the slimy marble.
We'll settle our accounts with fame among ourselves;
let socialism built in battle
be our common monument.

Descendant fishermen, watch the bobs of dictionaries;
from Lethe will float up debris of words
like *prostitution*,
            tuberculosis,
                blockade.
For you who are healthy and nimble
the poet licked up consumptives' spittle
with the rough tongue of posters.
With the tail of my years behind me
I look like those big-tailed, dug-up monsters.
Comrade life, let us beat our way
faster through the five-year-plan of remaining days.
Not a ruble have my verses brought me,
no mahogany furniture has been sent to my house.

In all conscience I need nothing,
except a freshly washed shirt.
When I appear before the C.C.C.* of clear bright years
ahead I'll raise—as my Bolshevik party card—
over the gang
                        of poet–profiteers,
the whole hundred volumes
                                    of my party-committed books.

—1930
TRANSLATED BY HENRY CARLISLE

In Full Voice (unfinished fragment)

The time: past one.
                        You've gone to sleep by now.
The Milky Way tonight
                        like a shining Oka streams.
I'm in no hurry.
                        Anyway, the telegram I'd send
would just disturb you.
                        As they say, the affair is over.
Love's craft is wrecked
                        on the shores of day-to-day.
We're finished, you and I.
                        How useless it would seem
to tally up a list
                        of every grief and pain
of all the hurtful things
                        we did to one another.

*The Central Control Commission (of the Communist party).

126

And look—there!

        What a glorious stillness in the world!

Night has set the sky out:

           a sheer homage of stars.

In hours like this, in perfect

             stillness, one should rise,

to address the Ages,

          History, the Universe. . . .

—1930

TRANSLATED BY ROSE STYRON

Marina Tsvetayeva and her daughter in 1916

MARINA
TSVETAYEVA

1892–1941

$\mathcal{M}$arina Tsvetayeva was born into an affectionate, cultivated Moscow family in 1892. Her father, the son of a
priest, was a self-made man. A Romance language professor, he was the founder of the Moscow Museum of Fine
Arts, known now as the Pushkin Museum of Fine Arts.
Marina's mother was a musician, and music was an important part of her childhood. When she was fourteen, her
mother died, and Tsvetayeva became quite independent.
A poor student in the gymnasium (high school), she was
absorbed in writing poetry. Her first book of poems was
published when she was still in school. The privately
printed *Evening Album* was a critical triumph. Two important Russian poets, Gumilev and Voloshin, hailed the
eighteen-year-old Marina as a peer.

In 1912 she married an attractive man her own age, Sergei
Efron, a member of a large and literary-minded Moscow
family of Jewish origin. During the Russian civil war, Efron
served on the side of the czarist armies. In 1922 the Efrons

129

emigrated—first to Prague and then to Paris, where they settled. They had two children, a boy and a girl.

For the Efrons, emigration turned out to be disastrous. Neither of them had any practical sense; they had to live in extreme poverty in a strange country. Tsvetayeva's attitude, proud, uncompromising, and also somehow capricious, alienated the *émigré* organizations and the editors of literary journals which could have helped her. One notable exception was the critic Marc Slonim, a lifelong friend who remained devoted to her despite her notoriously difficult disposition. He published a number of her poems in a distinguished socialist newspaper which he edited: *Volya Rossii* was printed in Russian in Paris during the twenties and early thirties.

Tsvetayeva and her family moved from one gloomy Paris suburb to another. Yet despite terrible material conditions, Tsvetayeva continued to write excellent poetry. Extremely prolific, she was unquestionably one of the great poets of her generation, using unerringly the enormous phonetic and semantic riches of the Russian language. Tsvetayeva is hard to translate into English precisely because of the melodic pioneering of her writings. Stripped of their sound patterns, her poems and even her occasional prose essays reveal at times an excessive romanticism. Her imagination, the freshness and daring of her perceptions, usually offset this weakness. Her technical mastery was instinctive—she maintained that she knew nothing at all about metrics. She was an important influence on modern Russian verse due to her metric innovations and her ability to convey effectively very personal, even intimate, experiences.

Tsvetayeva returned to Russia in 1938—and her return

home proved even more tragic than exile. In 1941, when the war broke out and the Russians started retreating before the Germans, Sergei Efron was shot, along with others in the USSR who were "politically unreliable" in the eyes of the police. Her son was killed in the first weeks of the war and her daughter was sent to a concentration camp. Tsvetayeva found herself utterly alone in the Soviet Union—this was the aftermath of Stalin's great purges of the mid-thirties: Russian intellectuals were terrorized. No one would have anything to do with a person returning from Europe—not Ilya Ehrenburg, an old friend, or even Pasternak who regarded Tsvetayeva so highly as a poet and as a person. On August 31, 1941, she hanged herself in the provincial town of Elabuga. She was buried there in a common grave. In the early sixties, in a period of relative liberalization in Soviet cultural matters, Tsvetayeva's verse began to be published in the USSR. She was rehabilitated posthumously and her works became immensely, incredibly popular almost overnight. Today she is beloved in her country, one of the significant lyric influences of the day.

Tsvetayeva's poetry is always passionate, youthful, dynamic. She was described by a faithful friend of hers, Olga Tchernoff (Olga Carlisle's grandmother) in a manner which conveys something of her vitality:

I met Tsvetayeva first in 1923, in Prague. Prague was a center for scholars and writers who were leaving Russia after the Revolution. The Czech government gave them stipends to live on, and funds for the publishing of Russian-language newspapers. I collaborated in one of them.

We had one room in a suburb of Prague—on a mountain in Smihov. On our second day there, someone knocked at the door.

131

A young woman came in—her brown hair in bangs, her light green eyes contrasting with her matte, dark skin. She was slender and stood erect with an almost unnatural straightness. Her brown dress was belted very tightly with a leather belt. Her waist was narrow and her shoulders bony.

"I am Marina Ivanovna Tsvetayeva-Efron," she says, extending her hand. Her hand is strong, a working hand, showing signs of age. On it she is wearing massive silver rings. She has silver manacle-like bracelets on her wrists. "We are neighbors. I wanted to meet you. . . . And then, I have a request. Could I borrow some knives and forks from you? We are having company tonight, and we haven't enough knives and forks!"

I am embarrassed. We have no silver either. We have just arrived. In Russia, we have exchanged all our possessions for bread. We have only two ancient silver spoons. For knives, we use a switch-blade Corsican knife, and a Corsican penknife with a Moor's head on one side of its handle and the inscription *Vendetta corsa* on the other. They are the relics of European traveling in another age. But Marina Ivanovna looks very pleased: "Corsican knives instead of kitchen knives! *Vendetta corsa!* You cut onions with them. Marvelous!" Her eyes shine. "It's morning now and I must go work—I *always* write in the mornings—but I hope to see you soon again."

Our friendship with Tsvetayeva and her husband and daughter grew rapidly. At that time our family was discovering Pasternak. Marina Ivanovna, for whom he was "a blow, a flight, a fall," was delighted. She had felt his greatness at once: "He is the most important now. Some modern writers *were*. Others *are*, but he alone is the future. He *will be*." Into lost Smihov, into a small room without chairs, without forks or knives, Pasternak's *Themes and Variations* would burst in:

Split your soul like wood. Let today froth to your mouth.
It's the world's noontide. Have you no eyes for it?
Look, conception bubbles from the bleached fallows;
Fir cones, woodpeckers, clouds, pine needles, heat.

TRANSLATED BY ROBERT LOWELL

Marina Ivanovna spoke about her own writing willingly. Rhythms lived in her powerfully, they were her soul, its emanation. It was impossible to say of her: "She mastered her art." Rather, her rhythms were her masters. They were her very breadth, accelerated, dazzling or thoughtful and lyric. She used to say: "The art of words is a pilgrimage along the sonorous paths of people and of nature." But

132

above all, in this pilgrimage she charted the course of her own feelings. She would read to us her most recent verse, still vibrating with the revolutionary storm.

The Cemetery

Slowly you walk, resembling me,
     directing low your eye.
So, looking down, I wandered once—
     Oh, pause here, passerby!

Read on my stone, your arms bouqueted
     with poppy, primrose, rue,
that I was called Marina
     and how many years I grew.

Forget this is a grave. Fear not
     I'll rise and show my face.
I loved, I cared too much, myself
     to tease in the wrong place,

and blood raced red beneath my skin,
     my hair curled round each day:
I lived. I too *was*, passerby!
     Passerby, oh, stay . . .

I can't accept eternity.
     Why was I buried? sealed?
I begged so not to go under the earth
     from my beloved field.

133

Pick for yourself a fragrant stem
      and then a wild strawberry;
the sweetest of the wild fruit grows
      in a green cemetery.

But only don't stand somberly,
      head down, a drooping bough—
think upon me lightly and
      lightly forget me now.

In the slant rays of the sun you glow,
      by powdered gold all crowned.
Do not be troubled should you hear
      my voice from underground.

—1911

TRANSLATED BY ROSE STYRON AND OLGA CARLISLE

A Red Cluster . . .

A red cluster—
the mountain ash had flared.
Leaves began to fall.
I was born.

There were quarrels of a thousand
tintinnabula.
It was a Sabbath Day
for St. John the Divine

Even now
I have that wish to gnaw
the bitter cluster
on the hot ash limb.

—1916
TRANSLATED BY ROSE STYRON

Lament with Me . . .

Lament with me as the morning nears
when bright no longer with thrones, fires, tears
these eyes which once incandescent ruled
by alien pennies shall be cooled
and a true countenance emerge, replace
its twin: my light but transient face.

I shall deserve to wear the sash
of proper comeliness at last.

And from afar, will I see you come
leading a long pilgrims' procession
down the dark path, and bewildered, stand
crossing yourself, taking then the hand
I've defended, kept, withdrawn before—
my hand which will be no more?

Living ones, I'll no longer spurn
your dearest kisses. I shall learn
not to be feverish, not to blush,

135

that 'round me peace may radiate a hush.
Veiled in grave beauty, head to toe
my Easter holyday I'll know.

Along the abandoned Moscow street I'll ride
and slowly you will walk beside
me. The first lump of earth will thud
loudly on the coffin's lid
and all will be resolved: the schemes,
the self-loving lonely dreams.

Lord, welcome one who life survived—
Lady Marina, newly arrived.

—1916
TRANSLATED BY ROSE STYRON AND OLGA CARLISLE

Soul, Scorning All Measure . . .

Soul, scorning all measure,
singer of heresy, martyr
longing for the whip's lashing.
Soul, you greet your assassin
like a butterfly fresh from its chrysalis.
Nor can you brook this offense:
that wizards are not still burnt.
Smoking under your hair shirt
like a resinate high wick,
screeching heretic,

136

sister of Savonarola,
Soul,
you deserve the stake!

—1921

TRANSLATED BY ROSE STYRON AND OLGA CARLISLE

Separation (for S. Efron)

Tighter and tighter wringing my hands
till they be riven—
Between us are not the miles of earth
but the rivers of heaven,
of separation, the azure lands
where my friend is forever
inalienable.

The highway dashes
in silvery harness;
my hands are not wrung now
but open, reaching
soundlessly,
like the mountain ash tree climbing
after a flight of cranes.

To fly like the cranes and not look back!
Haughtiness
would be mine, and in death's country
in costly dress

137

I would remain, to your fleet gold feathers
a last buttress
    in the airy losses of space.

—1921
TRANSLATED BY ROSE STYRON AND OLGA CARLISLE

Tousle-Haired Star

Tousle-haired star
hurrying into nothing
out of a crazy nowhere,
a lone sheep among the starry horde,
into those golden flocks rushing
like jealousy you overwhelm me,
star of the ancients, shaggy star!

—1921
TRANSLATED BY ROSE STYRON AND OLGA CARLISLE

Youth

Soon we will turn from swallows to the sorceress.
Youth, let us say good-by on this eve
of parting, sunburned, stand in the wind—
comfort your sister who grieves.

Flare the hem of your raspberry skirt,
my youth, my sunburned darling,
the deranger of my soul—comfort me,
dance, before our parting.

138

Fling your shawl of azure, wild one.
We've had our good times, you and I.
Now, dance, burn me, till morning breaks . . .
Amber and gold, good-by!

Not casually do I chance to touch you;
I say farewell as to a lover.
Torn from the tangled depths of the heart,
my youth, go on to others.

—1921
TRANSLATED BY ROSE STYRON AND OLGA CARLISLE

Poems to Czechoslovakia

O eyes full of tears
of wounds, of rage and love
Czechoslovakia weeping
Spain losing blood.

O black mountain cloud
eclipsing the world's sun
the time to return my ticket
to the Creator has come.

In this bedlam of nonpeople
I refuse to be alive.
Where wolves run in city squares
I refuse to live.

On backs bent submissively
I refuse to climb.
With sharks on the streaming plains
I refuse to swim.

I don't want ears
or eyes that cannot close.
To your universe of madness,
one answer: I refuse.

You shall not die, O Nation,
while God's still your advocate.
His blood made your garnets,
his breast bore you granite.

Advance! Be hard, O Nation, hard
as the Table of Laws—a vessel
red hot as garnets
lucid as your crystal.

—1939

TRANSLATED BY ROSE STYRON AND OLGA CARLISLE

OSIP
MANDELSTAM

1891–1938

How well I remember those remote, overgrown years of Russia, the decade of the nineties, softly slipping by in their unsalutary tranquillity and profound provincialism—a peaceful backwater, the last sanctuary of a dying era. At morning tea one listened to talk of Dreyfus, of the Colonels Esterhazy and Picquart, and to obscure arguments about some "Kreutzer Sonata." At the glass railroad station in Pavlovsk the change of conductors behind the tall podium always appeared to me as a change of dynasties. The frieze of silent newsboys on the corner . . . narrow droshkies . . . ladies with wide ballooning sleeves and wasp waists . . . the faces and hairstyles of gentlemen like the portrait gallery of some shabby barbershop . . . music in Pavlovsk . . . the center of the world.

from *The Noise of Time*

*A*s a child Osip Mandelstam could be seen strolling with his young French governess, a Christopher Robin with his Alice, along the streets of St. Petersburg. They would pause to regard the Winter Palace and the lights reflected in the River Neva. They would talk with the sentry at the statue of Nicholas I, admire the marine guards at their drill and the bemedaled majors guarding the Summer Garden

143

and the Royal Horse Guard parading on the day of the Annunciation. They would watch the students riot in front of the Kazan cathedral, the pomp of funerals by the Alexander Column. And they would stand at attention convincing themselves that silver trumpets, bugles, and drums heralded an attack of the cavalry. To the boy, it always seemed that "in Petersburg something very splendid and solemn was absolutely bound to happen." St. Petersburg was *his* city, a sacred world of beauty and order and enlightenment far from the depressing "chaos of Judaism," represented by the Talmudic books piled askew in the study of his merchant father, who had migrated to Russia from Warsaw when Osip was born. After he grew up, a slight, fine-featured impressionable young man with red hair and exceedingly long eyelashes, Mandelstam celebrated his city over and over again, in marvelous poetry and prose. He often called it by its Greek name, Petropolis:

> I am cold. A luminous Spring
> dresses Petropolis in green down.
> Like jellyfish, the light waves
> of the Neva disturb my calm.
> Along the northern river quay
> tiny firefly cars are hastening,
> dragonflies, and bugs of steel,
> and golden star-pins glistening.
> They cannot pierce, those stars of gold,
> the heavy sea waves' emerald.

and

> The dreams of earth catch fire on high,
> a green star shimmers, sighing—

144

Oh, if you are the star of water and sky
your twin, Petropolis, is dying. . . .

TRANSLATED BY ROSE STYRON AND OLGA CARLISLE

Young Mandelstam, educated in the best schools, had
a passion for the Russian language. He also loved French
and German literature, and traveling, and thus went off
to "read" in Paris, to study in Heidelberg. At twenty-two,
he published his first volume of poems, *Kamen* (*Stone*).
Neoclassic in form, elegant and profound, it shone with
intricate personal imagery and was hailed as a triumph in
Apollon, a leading journal of art and literature. Literary taste
was beginning to swing away from mystical Symbolism,
from Victorian fulsomeness. With the young poets Anna
Akhmatova and Nikolai Gumilev, Mandelstam sparked the
new Acmeist movement. The aim of the Acmeists (not
unlike that of the New Critics writing in English in the
1940s and 1950s) was to clarify and refresh poetry, to give
it concreteness, and to make its meanings precise. Poetic
style within the movement varied enormously. Mandelstam's was the most hermetic and verbally involved, but
never were the poems unclear. His images were consistent;
each word, each line with its stately, impeded rhythms had
that perfect balance of "intension" and "extension" the
New Critics would later extol. He admired Racine. He was
often inspired by architecture and other works of art, by
Homer, Dickens, and Poe.

Soon Mandelstam became a well-known personality in
St. Petersburg. His devoted friend Akhmatova describes
him as a brilliant conversationalist, witty, sharp-tongued,
intolerant of mediocrity, a man who wrote poetry of a

145

"divine harmony," a man "without poetic forebears." His wife Nadezhda, whom he adored and confided in, called him *zhizneradostny*—life-glad, endlessly bouyant and full of joy. Critics who had been wounded by his wit often abused him, but his second volume of verse, *Tristia*, published in 1922, brought him considerable fame. So did his autobiographical volumes, *The Noise of Time* and *Theodosia* (both 1925), and the novella *The Egyptian Stamp* (1928).

Mandelstam never opposed the October Revolution. He felt it was inevitable. But he did not enlist in the Red Army, and he was not drafted. He spent the war years largely in the south of Russia, most often in the Crimea, where other artists gathered. Once, in 1918, on a visit to Moscow, he became involved (at a place which sold sweets—Mandelstam's sweet tooth was legendary) in an incident with a notorious Chekist,* Blumkin, who was signing death warrants for alleged counterrevolutionaries. The poet grabbed the list from him, tore it up, and had to hide out in the snow-covered city. In 1920 he made his way back through Georgia to Leningrad where he stayed in a sanctuary for intellectuals called, in various writers' memoirs, "The House of Arts," or "The Mad Ship." Then he married Nadezhda, took on some assignments in translation and in journalism, went with his wife to Armenia, revisited Leningrad and the Crimea, and, finally, in 1933 was allocated an apartment in Moscow where he felt he would be more at the center of literary life. Just as their vagabond life seemed to end, the shadows of disaster fell across the Mandelstams' lives. Literary hostilities had been brewing

---

*A member of the Bolshevik secret police, the Cheka, now the NKVD.

146

and political persecutions were becoming widespread. In previous seasons (uncommonly often in May, it seemed—"Watch out, it is almost May!" his wife had teased the poet) there had been a number of arrests, a slow crescendo of oppression. Stalin had come to power and Mandelstam distrusted him. Never one to keep silent, he recited to a group of friends a poem he'd composed on Stalin:

> We live. We are not sure our land is under us.
> Ten feet away no one hears us.
>
> But wherever there's even a half-conversation,
> we remember the Kremlin's mountaineer.
>
> His thick fingers are fat as worms,
> his words reliable as ten-pound weights. . . .
>
> TRANSLATED BY ROBERT LOWELL AND OLGA CARLISLE

The version which somehow made its way to the police called Stalin "the murderer and peasant-slayer." In May 1934, there was a heavy knock at the Mandelstams' door, an all-night search through the apartment and its papers. At dawn, Stalin's secret police led the poet away while his wife and Akhmatova, who happened to be visiting, stood by.

There follows an appalling tale of prisons, insanity, exile, starvation. Some time after the first arrest, through Nadya's pleadings in "high places," Osip's sentence was commuted from forced labor on the White Sea Canal to exile in Cherdyn. His wife was allowed to accompany him, but his mind had been temporarily affected by his prison detainment, and he tried to commit suicide in Cherdyn, leaping from a hospital window. Nadya pleaded again and, to the amazement of his guards, Osip was allowed to choose another place of exile. He chose Voronezh, because he remembered hearing about it from a professor whose father was the prison doctor there. Voronezh turned out to be "a breathing space" for the Mandelstams. Friends aided them; the poet was allowed to work a bit at the local theater and broadcasting station, and once in a while he attended concerts for which he had written the program notes. They were still terribly poor, and Mandelstam could not publish, of course. Once Akhmatova came to visit them and wrote a beautiful poem called "Voronezh" ("And the whole city is impacted in ice. . . .").

In May 1937 their Voronezh exile ended and the Mandelstams were permitted to live in Kalinin, close enough to Moscow for occasional visits. "Moscow drew us like a magnet—we went there for gossip, news, money," the poet's wife remembers. They even managed a brief visit to Leningrad:

> I return to my city, dearer to me than tears
> to its veins, the swollen glands of childhood
>   nights,
> return. Swallow, o quickly then,
> the cod-liver oil of Leningrad's rivered lights. . . .
>
> I live on a back stairway; against my temple
> a constant doorbell strikes, torn from its flesh.
> And all night long I await our honored guests,
> shifting the heavy manacles of the door.

TRANSLATED BY ROSE STYRON AND OLGA CARLISLE

The once-joyous poet knew what was coming. Within the year, while he was a patient at a sanitorium not far from Moscow, Mandelstam was rearrested in what appeared to be a trap set by the secret police with the assistance of the Writers' Union. This time he was sent alone on a tortuous trip with other prisoners to Siberia to a concentration camp. The winter was dreadful and they stopped in Vladivostok at a transit camp. Here, freezing, starving (the poet imagined that he was being poisoned and refused even his meager rations), he died. The official date of his death was December 27, the day Yesenin hanged himself. A tender letter which through a miracle reached his wife was the last thing he wrote.

Much of Mandelstam's most powerful poetry was written far from St. Petersburg. As early as 1921, poems like "Concert at the Station"—a vision of Pavlovsk, the St. Petersburg suburb he lived in as a child—sound notes of foreboding. As his own tragedy developed, so did his conscience-stricken horror at the fate of his beloved Russia. Yet he never abandoned hope. Neither did his widow, who hid his papers and memorized his forbidden poems. No volume of Mandelstam's work has appeared in the USSR in nearly forty years; still he is considered by his peers to be supreme among Russia's twentieth-century poets.

O Sky . . .

O sky, sky, I will dream of you!
Surely you are not fully blind
And the day has not burned like a white page . . .
A trace of smoke, cinders on the ground.

—1911
TRANSLATED BY ROSE STYRON AND OLGA CARLISLE

I Shall Not See the Famous Phèdre

I shall not see the famous *Phèdre*
in the ancient theater crowned with tiers,
high in a smoke-blackened gallery
half-lit by melting chandeliers.
And while the players' vain graces
reap the sweet harvest of applause,
indifferent, I shall not hear their feathered
double-rhymes, borne light as gauze:

How those veils have wearied me . . .

Theater of Racine! A powerful barrier
separates us from another world;
Timed to its own deep-furrowed pulse
the giant curtain moves, unfurled.
And the classic mantle falls from their shoulders
and molten, suffering, their voice grows strong;
In the furnace of fury, tempered by grief,
the word is sounded: a red-hot gong.

I am late for the feast of Racine. . . .

150

Again the sere old posters rustle,
the scents of orange peel faintly rise,
and roused, as from a lethargy of years,
my neighbor returns to life and sighs:
"Melpomone's madness exhausts me so,
my thirst for present peace renews.
Let us go, before the spectator-jackals
come to tear apart the muse!"

If the Greeks could see our games . . .

—1915
TRANSLATED BY ROSE STYRON AND OLGA CARLISLE

In glass Petropolis we shall die,
our frail lives ruled by Proserpine.
Each breath sucks in the ruinous air
and the year on our graves each hour is known.

Goddess of the sea, thunderous Athene,
take off your helmet of potent stone.
In glass Petropolis, here we shall die
for you are not queen, but Proserpine.

—1916
TRANSLATED BY ROSE STYRON AND OLGA CARLISLE

To Cassandra

I did not look for, in moments of blossoming,
your lips, Cassandra,
Cassandra, your eyes.

151

But now a somber
December watches
and in remembrance torture lies. . . .

—1917
TRANSLATED BY ROSE STYRON AND OLGA CARLISLE

Because I Have Not Known . . .

Because I have not known how to keep your hands,
and I have betrayed your tender salty lips,
I must wait for dawn in this dense acropolis.
How I hate the weeping of the ancient logs.

The Achaean men in the dark prepare their horse,
with strong-toothed saws they cut into the walls.
There is no way to ease the dry agitation of the blood
and for you there is no name, no sound, no image.

That you'd return. How could I think this? How did
    I dare?
Why did I tear myself from you before our time?
Darkness has not dissolved, nor the rooster cried
and into the wood the hot ax has not yet sunk.

Like a transparent tear, on the walls resin emerges
and the city feels its scaffold wooden ribs;
Yet blood races toward the stairs now, assaults them
for three times heroes dreamed of the tempting Helen.

Where is fair Troy? What of the gilded palace?
It will be downed, that high birdhouse of Priam.
And the arrows fall like a dry wooden rain
and the arrows grow on the ground like chestnut trees.

The sting of the last star painlessly fades;
A gray swallow, morning taps at the window,
and the slow day, like an ox waking in straw
stirs through the squares, still rough from a long sleep.

—1920
TRANSLATED BY ROSE STYRON AND OLGA CARLISLE

I Have Forgotten the Word . . .

I have forgotten the word I wanted to say.
The swallow returns on its blind sheared wings
to the palace of shadows, to transparent friends—
In oblivion a night song is being sung.

The birds do not carol, nor the immortelle blossom,
the manes of the night horses fade from sight;
On the dry river an empty craft floats
and among the crickets, the word is lost.

Yet slowly it grows, as a tent, as a temple,
and now plays at being mad Antigone
or falls at my feet like a dying swallow
with Stygian tenderness and a twig of green.

153

Ah, to recapture those live seeing fingers!
The first recognitions—their sculpted joy!
I fear the weeping of Aonian maids,
the fog, the ringing, the void.

Our mortal power is passion and knowledge.
Through men's fingers flows even sound,
but I have forgotten what I meant to say
and the bodiless thought returns to the shadow land.

The shade keeps speaking, but her subject's wrong—
She's still the swallow, the flirt, Antigone,
and on my lips like a black ice burns
the remembrance of Stygian ringing.

—1920
TRANSLATED BY ROSE STYRON AND OLGA CARLISLE

A Stream of Gold Honey . . .

A stream of gold honey flowed from the glistening bottle
so thick and so slowly the hostess found time to remark
"Here where fate brought us, to melancholy Taurus,
we never are bored," and she looked over her shoulder.

Everywhere Bacchus is honored: to him who walks
it seems only guards and watchdogs still are living.
Like heavy barrels the tranquil days roll over;
unanswered, voices are heard from the far pavilion.

154

After our tea we strolled in the chestnut-brown garden;
the shades were lowered like eyelashes on the
  windows.
Past the white columns we walked, gazing at grapevines,
where sleepy mountains were drowned in airiest glass.

And I said, "the vines are arrayed like an ancient
  battle:
curly-haired horsemen ready in curving formation,
the science of Hellas lives on in stone-studded
  Taurus;
in golden acres, the noble rusted divisions."

As for the white room, silence waits like a spinning
  wheel;
it smells of vinegar, paint, of fresh wine from the
  cellar.
Remember in that Greek house the wife they all
  cherished—
not Helen, the other—remember how long she
  embroidered?

Golden fleece, fleece of gold, where shall you be
  discovered?
All the way here the falling sea waves droned,
and leaving his ship, its sails worn out by the voyage,
and filled with space and time Ulysses came home.

—1921

TRANSLATED BY ROSE STYRON AND OLGA CARLISLE

155

Concert at the Station

I cannot breathe; the solid earth wriggles with worms
and not a star speaks out.
Yet the gods know there is music aloft,
for the station trembles, the Aonians sing,
and, soon to be rent by the engine's whistle,
the air sleeps like a violin.

A gleaming park. The glass dome of the station.
Again the iron world is stunned to charm.
Solemnly the railroad car is being drawn
toward a sonorous feast, some foggy Elysium,
the crying of peacocks, the banging of grand pianos . . .
I am late. Afraid. A dream:

I enter now the crystal forest of the station,
the court of violins is in disarray
and the chorus of darkness wildly beginning,
and rotting in the greenhouse the roses smell.
Under a sky of glass the familiar shadow
hides all night in the crowd.

And to me it seems that in music and foam
the iron earth trembles like a beggar.
I push against the glass waiting room—
hot steam is blinding the violinist's bow.
Where are you going? At the feast in memory of a dear
    shadow
the music sounds for us a last time.

—1921
TRANSLATED BY ROSE STYRON AND OLGA CARLISLE

Tristia

I have studied the science of separation
between the tangled tresses of the night.
The oxen munch; longer than life this waiting,
the city's last hour vigil. Now the rite

of the rooster fills our daybreak—honor his cry
who lifts the burden of leavetaking man chooses:
eyes in sorrow fix on the distant horizon,
but the weeping of women is mixed with the singing of
    muses.

In the silence that hammers the word "separation,"
who can explain how each parting turns
or what is portended by the rooster's cry
when fire on the far Acropolis burns?

Or why, when the lazy oxen munch
in their stables, gazing at nothing at all,
the rooster, herald of some new life,
claps his wings on the city wall?

I love the simple spinning of thread—
the wheel skims and the spindle rides—
and look! on the air now, light as the down
of swans, a barefoot shepherdess glides . . .

How poor the foundations of our life!
How brief our language of joy, our vision.
All has come once, and will come again;
sweetest to us: the moment of recognition.

157

It shall be thus: a translucent figure
drawn like a flattened squirrel-skin stretching
on a clean argil plate, and bent there
over the wax, a young girl watching.

To fathom Erebus isn't for us.
Wax is to women as bronze to men. I
wager my life on the fields of battle
but she, telling fortunes, is destined to die.

—1921
TRANSLATED BY ROSE STYRON AND OLGA CARLISLE

Lord, This Night . . .

Lord, this night help me survive.
I'm frightened for my life, your slave.
To be in St. Petersburg alive
is to sleep in a long grave.

—1931
TRANSLATED BY ROSE STYRON AND OLGA CARLISLE

Ah, How We Loved . . .

Ah, how we loved
to deceive, to dream,
and now with ease
in the light forget
that we as children
were closer to death
than in our middle time.

158

The child of too little
sleep, of fever,
looked for an insult
on his plate,
but life is here—
I have no one to blame—
and I am alone, forever.

The animals
into the hillside blur,
the fish dart under
the farthest waves.
What folly to trace
the perplexing curves
of human passion and care!

—1932

TRANSLATED BY ROSE STYRON AND OLGA CARLISLE

Depriving Me of Sea . . .

Depriving me of sea, of a space to run and a space
   to fly,
And giving my footsteps the brace of a forced land,
What have you gained? The calculation dazzles,
But you cannot seize the movement of my lips,
their silent sound.

—1935

TRANSLATED BY ROSE STYRON AND OLGA CARLISLE

Under Such Blows . . .

Under such blows
your narrow shoulders will redden
and flame, even in the snow.

Your childlike hands
will lift up irons
and wave the heaviest ropes.

Barefoot on glass
your slight feet will go,
barefoot on glass in the blooded sand.

And I will burn for you
like a black candle
(a black candle). I shall not dare pray.

—1937

TRANSLATED BY ROSE STYRON AND OLGA CARLISLE

BORIS PASTERNAK

1890–1960

Boris Pasternak was born in Moscow, the eldest son of a well-known painter, Leonid Pasternak, who was a follower of Leo Tolstoy's teachings. His mother was a concert pianist. Anton Rubinstein, Scriabin, and Rainer Rilke were friends of the Pasternaks, a close-knit, cultivated family full of life and energy. As a child Pasternak wanted to become a composer; the well-known musician Scriabin was his idol. But Pasternak did not have perfect pitch, and he gave up music altogether at about twenty to study philosophy. An unhappy love affair then caused him to forget philosophy and to become a poet. "I think a little philosophy should be added to life and art by way of seasoning, but to make it one's specialty seems to me as strange as eating nothing but horse-radish," Lara, the heroine of *Doctor Zhivago*, says.

In the twenties Pasternak became recognized as one of the Soviet Union's greatest poets, though the daring of his poetic perceptions and of his forms always kept the average reader from appreciating him. He never ceased to write poetry, and in the thirties and forties, in years of repression when his work was seldom published, he earned his living with translations. He frequently traveled to Georgia in the Caucasus and his renderings of the Georgian poets, Shakespeare, Goethe, and Schiller are among the finest in the Russian language.

In 1958 the publication outside Russia of his *Doctor Zhivago* caused an extraordinary international scandal. The novel is by no means anti-Soviet—it is a romantic tale about a Russian poet (who is also a physician), living in Russia before and during the Revolution. Yet it caused Pasternak to be expelled from the Writers' Union, the professional association without which it is difficult for a writer to survive in the USSR. Pasternak was ostracized and abused in his own country while his fame abroad grew, but he is now the object of an ever growing, spontaneous popular cult in Russia. Like Pushkin's grave in Mikhailovskoye, near Pskov, Pasternak's grave in the Peredelkino cemetery near Moscow has become a nonofficial national shrine. For that reason, foreigners are discouraged nowadays from traveling to Peredelkino.

Pasternak's funeral was a memorable event. A Soviet poet wrote the following letter to Olga Carlisle about the funeral in the spring of 1960:

Much of Peredelkino was once a large estate belonging to the Samarin family.

. . . cold and dark behind the fence
A house whose beauty was marvel once
Stands. The heritage of the park is old:

164

Napoleon encamped here,
Here Samarin the Slavophile served out his life and was
   buried . . .*

The "house whose beauty was marvel"—the Church of the Transfiguration—is newly restored, its onion-shaped cupola now painted a
vibrant blue.

I reach the cemetery by walking along the railroad tracks, away from
the rustic railroad station. Along the gleaming tracks up on the hill
there is a switchman's shack guarded by a chained brown dog—
underneath, the Peredelkino cemetery.

A protective wall always encircles the Western cemetery, but Russian
graves are usually placed in complete disorder, while each individual
tomb is enclosed by a small wooden fence as if to say: "If there can
be no solitude in life, let there be some at least in the hereafter." Most
graves are marked by crosses but sometimes one sees a red obelisk
on the tomb of an unbeliever. . . .

I must tell you about Boris Leonidovich's funeral: On a sunny spring
day his open casket was brought here, carried on outstretched arms.
On the eve of Pasternak's funeral, leaflets began appearing on Moscow
walls, telling when the ceremony was to take place and how to get
to Peredelkino. They were torn off but more leaflets kept reappearing,
particularly in the neighborhood of the Kiev Station.

No Soviet writers of note were there, except for Konstantin Paustov-
sky. Mme. Ehrenburg attended in the absence of her husband who
was then in Stockholm. The funeral service had sent a car to take the
coffin to the cemetery, but Pasternak's family and friends disregarded
it. The pianist Svetoslav Richter played a Beethoven funeral march
on the poet's piano as the body was carried out of the house in a
profusion of spring flowers—in a heavy smell of lilac—high above the
heads of the crowd as was due to him. The great majority of the men
of letters then residing in the rest home did not attend the funeral.
During the procession I overheard a local Peredelkino *baba* [peasant
woman] grumbling: "They (the writers from the Union) have not
bothered to honor him . . . the cowards, we will not bother to go to
'their' funeral when the time comes." . . . One unfortunate aspect of
the ceremony was the indiscretion of foreign journalists who jumped
up and down and swung around in trees in their desire to catch a
more dramatic view of the funeral.

---

*From Boris Pasternak's "The Linden Alley," translated by Olga Carlisle.

After Pasternak's blossom-laden coffin was lowered into the grave, young men from the crowd started to read Pasternak's verse—they began with "Hamlet" from *Doctor Zhivago* which was taken up in unison by the whole assembly. Young poets took turns reading Pasternak's poems and their own dedicated to him, others made short speeches.

When a gaunt and poorly dressed man began a dull, religious-minded speech, the single official representative tried to stop him. A young man in workman's clothes pushed the representative aside, shouting: "Leave the speaker alone, this is not the Writers' Union here, you cannot stop us. . . ." The poetry reading lasted for hours and hours, late into a warm May night.

Down the hill, it is only a short distance to the poet's house. I walk along the fence of the Writers' Union Rest Home. Most of the wooden frame houses in Peredelkino belong to the Writers' Union and usually they are taken back from a writer's heirs two or three years after his death and given to another writer. Here is the gate which doesn't close tight, a graveled path leading to the house . . . in front of it the vegetable and flower garden which Pasternak cultivated himself.*

But it is a live Pasternak who remains with us, with his joie de vivre unparalleled in Russian literature:

I live with your picture, the one that is laughing,
whose fingers are twisting together as they
intertwine and bend back till the wrists are breaking—
whose guests settle sadly to stay and to stay.

Who from the cards' slapping, Rakoczy's bravado,
Crystal drops in the drawing room, glasses and guests,
Runs flaming, escaping along the piano,
From the corsets, the roses, the bones, the rosettes.

TRANSLATED BY AVRIL PYMAN

---

*Carlisle, *Voices in the Snow*, pp. 215–217.

His profound seriousness and his humility stay with us too:

> In everything I seek to grasp
>   the fundamental:
> the daily choice, the daily task,
>   the sentimental.
>
> To plumb the essence of the past,
>   the first foundations,
> the crux, the roots, the inmost hearts
>   the explanations.
>
> And puzzling out the weave of fate,
>   events' observer
> To live, feel, love, and meditate
>   and to discover.
>
> Oh, if my skill did but suffice
>   after a fashion
> In eight lines I'd anatomize
>   the parts of passion.

TRANSLATED BY AVRIL PYMAN

The Mirror

A cup of cocoa evaporates in the looking glass
and straight as an arrow, through sheer curtains,
    restless

167

into the faceted garden's alley, its trees in their
   chaos,
and on toward the empty swings the mirror rushes.

     Fair pines fill the air with the scent of
       resin
     and there a fenced-in greening garden
     has lost its spectacles in the grass,
     .and someone's shadow reads a book of verse.

     Toward the back, and the darkness behind
       the gate,
     and the steps, and the smell of sleepy
       sweet
     medicinal herbs in the garden aisles,
     flows hot shiny quartz amid twigs and
       snails.

Inside the room the great trees shake and toss
inside the mirror, yet never break the glass.
A collodion stream pours over, preserves each piece
from the stiff bureau to whispering trunks of trees.

     The mirror has flowed as mistless ice
     flows on the senses: the branch has lost its
     bitter taste, the smell of lilacs is almost
     gone, yet the trance persists.

The innumerable world sleepwalks with delicate
   gestures
and only the moving wind can dominate

what breaks into life, what breaks into light
only, refracting its play through a prism of tears.

> What can explode the soul? The earth's core
> eludes blasting and digging like deep-hid
>   treasure.
> Inside the room the great trees shake and
>   toss
> inside the mirror, yet never break the
>   glass.

Under the spell of this land of my belonging
there is nothing that extinguishes my vision.
Thus, after rain, the open eyes of the garden
statues are crossed by garden slugs, slithering,

and water runs over their ears, and siskins
chirruping hop on their toes. You may blacken
their stone lips with blueberries; still
you can't inebriate their souls.

> Inside the room the huge garden carouses,
> raises a fist at the mirror to harass,
> runs to the moving swing, catches and
>   clouds it,
> and shakes that fist, and does not break
>   the glass.

—1917
TRANSLATED BY ROSE STYRON AND OLGA CARLISLE

Illness

One way or another it can happen:
at some unsuspected, fixed-on moment,
more stifling than clerics droning, night-
black monks, illness may pounce on you.

Frost. Night at the window, looking,
as is its practice, after the ice thickening.
Wrapt in furs, curled in a roomy armchair,
a spirit purrs away, a pure monotony.

A bough in profile, offering its cheek,
the parquet floor, and the poker's shadow
out of drowsing and remorse highlight
the daylong, lunatic-raving blizzard.

The night is still, the ice-clear night.
And like a blind whelp lapping milk,
among fir trees, sunk in their own
gloom, the pickets lick away at starlight.

Is it the fir trees' thawing gleams,
a candle guttering wildly in the night?
Flicking its paw, the snow blinds fir on fir.
The tree-hollows shadow deeper hollows.

This quiet, this sky crouched down,
the telegraph's waves swelling toward elegy,
did they strain after the cry, "Answer!"
or was it some other silence echoing?

Deafness alone among the twigs and needles,
deafness among the tongue-tied spheres.
That flicker seems the only answer
in the air to someone's lingering call.

Frost. Night at the window, looking,
as is its practice, after the ice thickening.
Wrapt in furs, curled in a roomy armchair,
a spirit purrs away, a pure monotony.

But his lips! Bitten till they bleed.
He's trembling, his face locked in his hands.
That chalk-white face, those gestures augur
a storm of wonder for him come after.

—1918–1919
TRANSLATED BY THEODORE WEISS

1905 (a fragment)

The throbbing of drums
drowns in the roar of the railroad,
the scraping of wheels
on the executioner's cart
drowns in the sharp harangue
from the speaker's platform:
Russia, the land of serfs,
acclaims its reforms!

171

The First of March. Perovskaya.
The Will of the People*—
pince-nezed students,
Nihilists in workers' clothes.
The tales of our fathers
sounding like reigns of the Stuarts,
farther away than Pushkin,
the figures of dreams. . . .

Here Dostoevsky came,
and the faithful women.
Who guessed each search
would yield a museum relic?
They readied themselves
for death, oblivion, Nechaev
who buried their beauty from mankind,
underground.

And were it yesterday
thirty years gone, and, strolling
I'd lit that door
with my flickering kerosene,
the young girls bent in the dark there,
warrior-chemists
with their bombs, would be
my mother and her friends.

—1926
TRANSLATED BY ROSE STYRON AND OLGA CARLISLE

*The Will of the People was a secret terrorist organization which succeeded in
assassinating Czar Alexander II on March 1, 1881. Perovskaya and Nechaev were
members of this organization.

Early Trains

. . . And, as in church, I humbly watch
those I revere: old peasant women,
workers and simple artisans,
young students, men from the countryside.

I see no traces of the yoke
born of unhappiness or want.
They bear their daily trials
like the masters. They have come to stay.

Fixed in every sort of posture,
sitting in groups, in quiet knots
the children and the young are still,
reading, engrossed like wound-up toys.

Then Moscow hails us in a mist
of darkness, silver gray.
And leaving the subway station
we come into the light of day,

The young are pressed against the railing
They smell of soap and honey cakes.

—1941
TRANSLATED BY OLGA CARLISLE

173

Hamlet

The applause is over. I step out from the wings.
Leaning against the door frame, I listen
to the dying echoes, life outside the stage,
and try to figure what, in mine, will happen.

Under its arch of darkness night stares and
magnifies me. A thousand pairs of starry
opera glasses burn. Abba, Father, if you can find
a reason, this once let the cup pass me by.

I love your stubborn, difficult designs,
and I'm content to play the role I've drawn,
but tonight let me out of it, let me be.
Tonight another drama's going on.

The acts in sequence are thought out, rehearsed.
The trail of days narrows, its end is sealed.
I am alone here, drowning among the Pharisees.
To live a life is not to cross a field.

—1945
TRANSLATED BY ROSE STYRON

Winter Night

The snow swept through the land
to the ends of the earth.
On the table a candle,
a candle was burning.

174

Like moths in the summer
attracted by flames,
crowding and rushing
—snowflakes at the window.

The blizzard had drawn
white circles and arrows.
On the table a candle,
a candle was burning.

Shadows softly mingling
on the luminous ceiling,
arms and legs intertwining,
destinies crossing.

Two tiny slippers
fell to the floor,
and the candle was weeping
wax tears on her dress.

All was lost in the darkness,
snowy and gray.
On the table a candle,
a candle was burning.

The candle was almost
put out by a draft.
The heat of temptation
raised its wings like an angel.

175

A February blizzard,
lasting a month.
On the table a candle,
a candle was burning.

—1946–1953
TRANSLATED BY OLGA CARLISLE

ANNA AKHMATOVA

1889–1966

$\mathcal{A}$nna Andreyevna Akhmatova was essentially a poet from St. Petersburg. The refinement, the dignity of her verse are representative of that most orderly and European of Russian cities. Akhmatova became famous in 1912, when her first book, *Evening,* was published. The intense feminine tone of her early love poems was widely, though unsuccessfully, imitated in Russia for years.

As a very young woman Akhmatova joined the Acmeists, an exclusive poets' guild which emphasized poetic craft. This group included two other important poets of that time—her husband Nikolai Gumilev and Osip Mandelstam, a lifelong friend. The Acmeists were dedicated to freeing Russian verse from Victorian rhetoric: dominant then in the Petersburg literary world was a group of poets known as the Symbolists, who were mystically inclined, often mannered and obscure. The Acmeists on the other hand wanted, in the poet Mandelstam's words, to reinstate "the power of the word itself," because "each word is a

179

psyche, a live soul choosing its own sweet body." Akhmatova and Mandelstam remained faithful to the Acmeist precepts all their lives—and their poems are among the greatest achievements of Russian literature.

This is how Anna Akhmatova described her own life, in a preface to her *Selected Poems*, which was published in Moscow in 1961. This preface, written in a restrained tone typical of the late Akhmatova, is entitled "A few words about myself." It is interesting to see how traditional her upbringing and education had been. The key to her achievement surely lies in part in her total dedication to her art. She set it above her private life, above any comforts or immediate fame that may have tempted her.

I was born on the twenty-third of June in the year 1889 at Bolshoi Fontan near Odessa. At this time my father, a former mechanical engineer with the Navy, was retired. As a child I was taken North, first to Pavlovsk, then to Czarskoye Selo,* where I lived until I was sixteen.

My first recollections are of Czarskoye Selo: the wet, green splendor of the parks; the pasture where my nurse used to take me; the hippodrome where colorful horses pranced; the old train station.

I spent every summer on Streletsk Bay near Sevastopol, and there became friends with the sea. My strongest impression of those years is the ancient city of Hersones, near which we stayed.

I learned to read with the primer Leo Tolstoy wrote. At the age of five, hearing the teacher giving French lessons to the older children, I learned to speak it with them.

I wrote my first poem when I was eleven. My consciousness of poetry did not awaken with Pushkin and Lermontov but with Derzhavin ("On the Birth of an Imperial Child") and Nekrassov ("Frost the Red-nosed"), poems which my mother knew by heart.

I attended the girl's Gymnasium at Czarskoye; first I did badly, then much better, but always unwillingly. I did my last year at Fundukleyev Gymnasium in Kiev, from which I graduated in 1907.

---

*Imperial towns near Leningrad, famous for their magnificent palaces, which were country residences for the czars before the Revolution.

I enrolled in the law school of the Women's University at Kiev. As long as I was studying law history and, in particular, Latin, I was satisfied, but when it came to purely legal matters I began to feel cold toward my subjects. Moving, then, to Petersburg, I followed Rayev's advanced courses in history and literature. At that time I was already writing poetry regularly. When I was shown the proofs of Innokenty Annensky's* *The Cyprus Chest* I was thunderstruck and read it oblivious of everything else in the world.

In 1910 the crisis in Russian Symbolism was apparent, and the new poets no longer joined this movement. Some involved themselves with Futurism, others with Acmeism. I became an Acmeist.

I spent two springs, in 1910 and 1911, in Paris, where I witnessed the first triumphs of the Russian ballet. In 1912 I traveled through northern Italy—Genoa, Pisa, Florence, Bologna, Padua, Venice. Italian painting and architecture made a tremendous impression on me. They were like a dream one has known all one's life.

In 1912 my first collection of poems appeared, called *Evening*, of which only 300 copies were printed. It was received benevolently by the critics. In 1914 my second book, *Rosary*, came out.

I spent every summer in what had formerly been the Tver province, a place ten miles from Bezhetsk. It was not a picturesque landscape: hilly fields ploughed in regular squares, mills, marshes, half-drained swamps, gates, wheat, wheat . . . There I wrote almost all of *White Flight*; it was published in September, 1917.

Following the October Revolution I worked in the library of the Institute of Agronomy and did editorial work for various publications. In 1921 my collection *The Plantain* appeared, and in 1922 *Anno Domini*.

Starting in the middle twenties I studied very assiduously and with intense interest the architecture of old Petersburg and the life and works of Pushkin. The result of my Pushkin investigations was three works: one on *The Golden Cockerel*, another on Benjamin Constant's *Adolphe*, and another on *The Stone Guest*. Each of these studies was published in its day. I am now preparing a book called *The Death of Pushkin*.

When war came in 1941 I was in Leningrad. At the end of September, when the city was already blockaded, I flew out of Leningrad to Moscow.

Until May 1944 I lived in Tashkent, where I avidly seized upon news from Leningrad and the front. As did other poets, I often visited hospitals to give readings of poetry to wounded fighting men. In the burning heat of Tashkent, I learned for the first time what the shadow

---

*A very influential, hermetic writer who belonged to the Symbolist movement.

181

of a tree, the sound of running water can mean. Also in Tashkent I learned what human kindness is, for I was often seriously ill there.

In May 1944 I flew to springtime Moscow, already full of joyous hope and expectations of an imminent victory. In June I returned to Leningrad.

Years before I had become absorbed by the problems of artistic translation. After the war I did a lot of translation. I was particularly interested in ancient Korean poetry and popular Serbian epics.

The reader of my poems will see that I have never stopped writing poems. In them lies my link to our time, to the new life of my people. As I wrote them I lived with the very rhythms that resounded through the heroic history of my land. I am happy to have lived in these years and to have seen events without equal.

Though she could not say so in her autobiography, Akhmatova's life, like that of many Russians of her generation, was a difficult one ("Like a river, I was turned around/by a stern epoch"). Her former husband, Nikolai Gumilev, was shot by the Bolsheviks in the early twenties. Her son was sent to Siberia. She herself lived through many years of anguish and hardships during the post-World-War-II wave of cultural repression. Nonetheless until her death Akhmatova grew steadily as an artist, never ceasing to write. During a period of cultural "thaw" in 1965 she was allowed to go abroad twice—to Italy and to Oxford, to receive an honorary degree there. In her late years, she was a symbol of nobility and courage for her countrymen. Her popularity among young readers was enormous—she was identified with the Russian intellectuals' struggle for more freedom.

The Gray-Eyed King

The crown is yours, old tyrant pain!
Tonight our gray-eyed king is gone.

My husband, returning, said with calm:
"The autumn dusk was airless, crimson,

> under an ancient oak they found him,
> up from the hunt they carried him home.

> He was so young . . . I pity the queen . . .
> All white in an evening her hair's become."

He finds his pipe on the mantelpiece
and out again to his night job goes.

Now I shall awaken my daughter,
search her deep gray eyes

> and show her, flying the castle tower
> the flag that mourns her father's death

> while constant poplars at the window thrum
> "Your king is no longer on earth."

—1916
TRANSLATED BY ROSE STYRON

Bezhetzk

There are white churches there, and ringing, luminous
   ice.
The blue eyes of my son are blossoming there.
Over the ancient city Russian night is a diamond,
and the scythe of the moon is as yellow as honey.

183

Dry winds come up from the fields by the river,
and men are like angels, rejoicing at Christmas.
The room is clean, the icon lights are lighted,
on the heavy table the Scriptures are open.
There, stern memory, miserly now,
for me with a bow opened its rooms.
But I did not go in. I slammed the door hard,
and the city was filled with holiday bells.

—1921
TRANSLATED BY OLGA CARLISLE

A Fabulous Autumn . . .

A fabulous autumn built itself a high dome.
The clouds were ordered to leave it undarkened.
People marveled: the September deadlines have
    expired—
Where did the cold, damp days disappear?
The water turned emerald in the murky canal;
And nettles smelled stronger than roses.
The dawns left us breathless; they were red and
    demonic,
We'll remember them as long as we live.
The sun was a rebel storming a city,
And spring-like autumn caressed him so wildly
that we looked for gleaming, transparent snowdrops.
This is when, calmly, you walked to my door.

—1922
TRANSLATED BY OLGA CARLISLE

184

Voronezh

And the whole city is impacted in ice.
Under a glass lie trees, walls, snow.
I walk on crystal hesitantly;
unsure of its run
                the ornamented sleigh.
In Voronezh, crows trim Peter's statue
near the frozen poplars, a green arcade
washed pale by the light,
                    lost in a sunny dust.
Its hills remember Kulikovo's battle,
where the power of Earth was crowned victorious,
and the poplars raise their frosted goblets
and chime against the sky
like guests
          drinking a thousand toasts
at a bridal feast, we are honored.
But in the room of the punished poet
Fear and the Muse watch, in turn,
as night falls
          and there is no hope of dawn.

—1936

TRANSLATED BY ROSE STYRON AND OLGA CARLISLE

Two Poems

Dreary are the triumphs
of famed non-meetings—
phrases unspoken

185

words unrelating
glances that know
neither contact nor rest
only tears relieved
to be flowing—Alas!
a wild briar-rose
from the environs of Moscow
figures in all this they'll call
Immortal Love.

"You are with me again, autumn, my friend!"
—*I. Annensky*

In the garden of Paradise others may bask
on southern holidays, still,
but here I choose autumn for my friend
where it's northerly and chill

For here I guard the blest memory
of my last non-meeting with you
and the pure cold light of my conquest
of fate hallows my view.

—1956

TRANSLATED BY ROSE STYRON

186

1913

> In Petersburg we will meet again
> as if we had buried the sun there. . . .
> —*O. Mandelstam*

> That was the last year.
> —*M. Lozinsky*

Christmastide, candescence of bonfires
   bridges parting to topple the carriages
      the whole city in funeral procession floats
downstream, or upstream, borne on the Neva
   toward undetermined harbors somewhere,
      a destination far from its roots.
Black-arched silhouette in Galérnya
   weathervane shrill in the Summer Garden
      and over Russia's Age of Silver
         a silver moon grows cold,
for, unobserved, a shadow's moving
   slowly moving along the embankment
      nearing every threshold on the road.
From walls a wind, ripping the posters
   whirling the smoke in a dance of rooftops
      and all the lilacs of graveyards smell,
and banished, bewitched like Czarina Avdotya*
   Dostoyevskyan, the unearthly
      city vanishes under a fogged veil . . .
And reappears, out of the darkness—
   Petersburg, the old carouser!

---

*Avdotya is a popular form of the Russian name Eudoxia. Czarina Avdotya was Peter the Great's first wife, whom he compelled to take the veil.

187

Drums beat as they did for executions.
And under the stifling frosty air
in the lecherous sinister pre-war air
hung the sound of revolutions.
A hollow howling—oh, barely heard,
drowning itself in snowdrifts hoarded
along the Nevsky boulevard,
like a man possessed of demonic fevers
on some dreadful night reflected in mirrors
refusing to see where his likeness lives
while down the legendary embankment
oblivious to the world's calendar
the true twentieth century arrives.

—1940–1962
TRANSLATED BY ROSE STYRON AND OLGA CARLISLE

ALEXANDER BLOK

1880–1921

Because of his extraordinary insights into a changing Russia, Alexander Blok is widely regarded as her first major modern poet. Surely he is the finest Russian lyric poet of his time.

Early in his career, Blok wrote beautiful love poems—to women, to an imaginary Neoplatonic "Beautiful Lady," to Russia, to the cities he visited. His voice was always full of compassion. Thus this short poem about Petersburg laments the fate of an abandoned sailor:

> In the late autumn
>   the quay white with snow,
> Out from the harbor
>   the heavy ships go—

and they leave behind a poor sailor, who can only lie down in the thin snow and die:

191

Most pure, most tender
  winding sheet
Wrapped in it, sailor,
  is your sleep sweet?

Blok was beloved in pre-Revolutionary Russia. A romantic figure—handsome, gray-eyed, generous—he was an idol of the literary salons and a hero to his readers. He had a metaphysical turn of mind, and he exerted a profound influence on the younger poets of the day. He was an accomplished essayist, opening up the literary, philosophic, and social issues of his day to brilliant scrutiny.

As the Revolution neared, Blok's writings began to change, to foreshadow the end of an era, and the rise of another—urban and increasingly barbarous. Blok's sense of his country's historic destiny is best illustrated in his poem, "The Scythians," where he describes Russia's geographic and political dilemma, lying as it does between China and the West.

In 1918 Blok wrote a long poem which became famous overnight. In form, it is somehow reminiscent of the works of the English Imagists of the twenties. It is called "The Twelve" for the twelve Red Army men lead by Christ himself who are marching through a frozen, frightened city—nighttime Leningrad during the civil war. The symbolism of this poem is ambiguous. Is the poet celebrating the October Revolution? Does Christ condone the oppressive rule of the Bolsheviks? Will He redeem them?

Blok's love and understanding of Russia were those of a mystic. He had been a Socialist—never the orthodox, dogmatic kind—and he had both feared and welcomed the oncoming Revolution. In 1921, still young, Blok died. He was gasping, as it were, for air, more depressed by visions of violence to come than by the hardships of the civil war. His funeral, like that of Pushkin before him and of Pasternak after him, was a manifestation of public grief.

Shortly before he died, on August 7, 1921, Blok made a public speech to commemorate the 84th anniversary of the death of the poet Alexander Pushkin.

Some of his words sounded like a warning: in the early twenties, Russian culture was entering into a new, autocratic age, but the artist's right to his inner freedom had to be reasserted if art was to survive in Russia:

In the memory of our childhood, a joyful name lives on: that of Pushkin. It is a proud sound, this name, enough to fulfill many a day in our lifetime. Dark are the names of emperors, great captains, inventors of assassinating instruments, of hangmen, of the martyrs of life. A bright name stands beside these: Pushkin.

Pushkin bore his solemn burden with ease and gaiety, and yet the role of a poet is neither easy nor gay; it is tragic. Pushkin played the role as a grand master, sure, free, and with a broad control. Yet our heart is often torn at the thought of Pushkin: the poet's joyful march of triumph, which traveled on nothing of the outer world, was too often hindered by those somber men who hold that a kettle is more precious than God.

In the man Pushkin we see a friend of monarch and Decembrists. Let Pushkin the poet appear, and all else vanishes.

The poet has a permanent standing: his language and his habits may age, but the essence of his work will never age.

Men of the world may turn away from a poet and his work. Today they build him a monument; tomorrow they seek to "drop him from the ship of actuality." But this is of interest only to the men of the world. The poet lasts. The essence of poetry, as of all art, is permanent; whether men adopt one attitude or another concerning poetry is in the end a matter of indifference.

Today we honor the memory of Russia's greatest poet. It seems right to speak at this time about the calling of the poet, grounding my words on Pushkin's own ideas.

What is a poet? A man who writes verse? Surely not. He is not called a poet for writing verse; yet he writes in verse, that is, he harmonizes words and sounds because he is a son of harmony, a poet.

And what is harmony? Harmony is the concord of universal forces, the universal order of life. Order is the Cosmos, opposed to disorder—Chaos. Out of Chaos, according to the ancients, the Cosmos came into being—into peace. The Cosmos is the kin of Chaos as the sea's unbroken waves are the kin of the ocean's turbulence. A son may differ from his father in all things, save for a hidden trait; but that trait will cause the son to resemble his father.

Chaos is elemental and primitive anarchy; the Cosmos, ordered harmony, culture; from Chaos the Cosmos came into being; the element contains in itself the seeds of culture; out of the inorganic, harmony comes into being.

Universal life is the perpetual creating of new forms. They sleep in the cradle of inorganic chaos; they grow and undergo selection through culture; harmony gives them their contours, and these in turn disappear into the mist of the inorganic. The sense of this movement is indeed beyond our understanding, its essence obscure; we take our solace from the thought that a new form is better than an old: but the wind extinguishes our feeble light illuminating the universal darkness. Order in the world is truly terrifying: it is the son of disorder, and need not coincide with our notions of good and evil.

We know but one thing: a form that replaces another form is new; the form replaced is old; we witness everlasting changes in the world; we ourselves play a part in this fluctuation of forms and types, a part that is mostly passive; we degenerate, grow old, and die; we rarely ever play an active part, and only then by taking a place in universal culture, and by working to build new forms.

A poet is the son of harmony; a part in the universal harmony belongs to him.

Three tasks pertain to the poet: first, he has to free his sounds from the primitive and inorganic element in which they live; next, he must set them into harmony, giving them form; and finally, he must introduce this harmony into the outer world. . . .

The labors of a poet concern the general culture, as is said nowadays; his activity is historical. He can therefore declare, after Pushkin:

> It matters not to me if the press
> Freely confuses the fool,
> Nor if the careful censor restricts
> In the pages of magazines
> The place of the poorer wits. . . .

194

In speaking thus, Pushkin asserts the right of the plebeian—of the people—to establish censorship, since he admits that the number of fools will never grow smaller.

It is not the task of the poet to battle incessantly with fools; to the contrary, his harmony effects a selection among them, attracting from the mass of human waste a thing more interesting than mere humanity. Early or late, true harmony will find its goal: no worldly censor can oppose this essential calling of the poet.

On a day devoted to the memory of Pushkin, we shall not argue whether he drew a careful distinction between what we call "personal" and "political" liberty. We know that he called for "another," "mysterious" liberty. For us it is "personal," but for the poet it isn't merely so:

> To reckon with no one else,
> serving and pleasing one's self.
> To hold, among lackeys and kings,
> both head and conscience erect.
> To walk about at one's ease,
> delighting in holy nature
> and works of inspired art.
> To sink in tender silence!
> There is my justice, and joy. . . .

Pushkin wrote this on the eve of his death. He said the same thing in his youth:

> Love and mysterious liberty
> raise in my heart a simple hymn. . . .

But the closer his life drew to its own end, the more cumbersome the barriers placed in its way. Pushkin grew weak, and the culture of his time grew weak along with him—Russia's one great period of culture in the last century. The fatal forties approached. On Pushkin's bed of death the infantile stammerings of Bielinski* were first heard. These stammerings seemed openly at odds with the polished voice of Count Beckendorff.† And it seems so even today. It would be altogether too tragic if it seemed otherwise. And even if it were otherwise, we would persist in thinking that it was not.

---

*A well-known critic.

†Chief of Police whose secret agents are said to have arranged the duel in which Pushkin lost his life; the czar wanted to get rid of Pushkin because of his liberal ideas and his great popularity.

Pushkin did not die by a bullet from D'Anthés' pistol. He died for lack of air. The culture died with him.

> Friend, it is time for us to rest. . . .

So Pushkin sighed before his death; so, too, his cultural era.

> Happiness is lacking in the world,
> but peace it knows, and liberty. . . .

Peace and liberty—these are essential to the poet for the liberation of harmony. Yet these can vanish too. Creative happiness, not outer happiness. Not the freedom of a child—the liberty to act as a liberal—but creative freedom, secret freedom. And the poet dies for want of air to breathe; life has lost its sense. . . .

TRANSLATED BY RICHARD RAND

Ravenna

All that is transient, all that is frail
you've locked in each century's tomb
and you sleep as a child, Ravenna,
in the drowsy arms of time.

No longer shall slaves mosaics bring
here through the Roman gate;
on the walls of your cool basilicas
the gilt is wearing out

and the rough vaults of sepulchers
grow soft with moisture's kiss,
and mold veils the sarcophagi
of holy monks and empresses

196

and silent are your burial halls,
their thresholds dark at dawn,
lest blessed Galla's black eyes waking
burn through the cold stone.

A bloody history, war and hurt,
have been erased, forgotten:
Placidia's voice shall not revive
to sing of bygone passion,

and the sea has far receded,
and roses the ramparts charm
lest Theodoric in his tomb
asleep should dream life's storm.

All the people and houses, the vine-hung
wastes are graves. The bronze
splendor of Latin inscriptions sounds
a lone trumpet on the shrines.

And only in the pure, tranquil gaze
of a fair Ravenna maiden
regret for the sea that can never return
glimmers now and then

and only at night, accounting the centuries-
to-come, bent over this valley,
does the aquiline profile of Dante's ghost
sing of the New Life to me.

—1909

TRANSLATED BY ROSE STYRON

197

The Scythians

You are but millions—we are an infinite number.
Measure yourselves against us, try.
We are the Scythians, we are the Asians you call us
with slanted and greedy eye.

Centuries of your days are but an hour to us,
yet like obedient guards
we've held a shield between two hostile races:
Europe and the Mongol hordes.

Hundreds of years go by, still you look eastward,
collecting, melting our pearls,
and laughing at us as you wait for the ripe moment
to blast our walls.

But time has come to term and the evil hour
beats its wings. Each day multiplies
offenses; soon of your lovely Paestums
there will be no trace.

To love the way our blood can love—
Have those long days
since you forgot the way rendered you blind
to love that burns, destroys?

These we still love: the fever of cold numbers,
the gift of heavenly visions.
And these we know: the piercing Gallic wit,
Germany's somber genius.

198

And we remember a Paris street's inferno
and the damp freshness of Venice,
the smell of distant lemon groves
and Cologne's spired smokiness.

The flesh, we crave—its taste, color,
its heavy deadly smells.
Is it our crime if your frail skeletons
crumble in tender paws?

Through time, we have caught the bridles of playful
stallions, taught them to be unwild.
We've broken the backbones of unruly horses
and slave-girls who rebelled.

From war and horror come to our open arms,
the embrace of kin,
Put the old sword in its scabbard while there's
time, hail us as friends.

Lest, along the plains and forests, before
the comely European race,
We open ranks, and bound by no promise,
show our Asiatic face.

Yes, come, stream to the Urals where we'll clear
the battle site you'll need
for steel machinery with calculated breath
to meet the horde.

But we, we will no longer shield you
nor fight at all,
content observing with our narrow eyes
the death-brew boil.

Nor shall we flinch to see the ferocious Hun
pillage each corpse,
herd all his horses into church and burn
mounds of white flesh.

Ah, Old World, before you have perished, join
our fraternal banquet. Hear
perhaps for the last time summoning you
the barbaric lyre!

—1918
TRANSLATED BY ROSE STYRON AND OLGA CARLISLE

The Twelve (fragments)

Our sons have gone
to serve the Reds
to serve the Reds
to risk their life.

O bitter, bitter pain,
sweet life!
a torn overcoat!
an Austrian gun!

—To get the bourgeois
We'll start a fire
a world-wide fire, and drench it in blood—
the good Lord bless us. . . .

O you bitter bitterness,
boring boredom
deadly boredom.

This is how I will
spend my time.

This is how I will
scratch my head,

munch on seeds,
sunflower seeds,

play with my knife
play with my knife.

You bourgeois, fly as a sparrow!
I'll drink your blood,

your warm blood, for love,
for dark-eyed love.

God, let this soul, Your servant, rest in peace.

Such boredom! . . .

201

Thus they march through the night,
all twelve, on and on.
They are without pity,
without icon.

Their steel rifles are seeking
the invisible foe.
in the dark side streets,
in the deepest snow.

A red flag is flapping
across their eyes.
Their rythmic marching
goes on and on.

The fierce enemy
will be coming soon.
The snow is blinding them.
they are marching on,

Day and night.

"Power to the People!" . . .

The Twelve step steadfastly.
"Who's there? Come out!"
It's the wind which is playing
with a red flag.

The snowdrifts are icy.
"Come on out from the drift!"
But they are followed only
by a hungry dog.

"Get away, else we'll get you
with our bayonets!"
The Old World is no better
than a mangy old dog.

Hungry wolf,
he will follow
baring his teeth.
"Who goes there?"

"Who is there in the distance
waving a flag?
In the darkness rushing,
by the shadow of walls?

Never mind, we'll get you!
Better give yourself up!
Comrade, we'll kill you.
Come on out or we'll shoot!"

Only an echo,
From beyond the walls.
Only the laughing
of the huge snowstorm.

And they march steadfastly,
a dog trailing behind—
while ahead—
with a bloody red flag,
unseen in the snow,
immune to their bullets
in a scattering of snowy pearls,
in a crown of white roses,
our Lord
is walking
with a tender step.

—1918
TRANSLATED BY OLGA CARLISLE

1613
Romanovs elected to power. Michael Romanov becomes czar: Moscow.

1689–1725
Peter the Great westernizes Russia, builds navy and reorganizes army, defeats Sweden, builds St. Petersburg.

1703–1918
St. Petersburg is the capital and cultural center of Russia, influenced by European ideas, architecture, art.

1726–1796
Catherine the Great advances westernizing of Russia, introduces French culture. She also creates new problems of serfdom by laws attaching peasants to the land as saleable property. Poland defeated, Crimea conquered.

1773
Cossack-serf uprising, led by Pugachev, fails.

1801–1825
Alexander I annexes Finland, Bessarabia, and Georgia, initiates Caucasian wars, becomes important figure at Congress of Vienna, furthers culturalization of young Russians.

1812
Napoleon invades Russia, is driven back. Russians march into Paris.

1825
Decembrist uprising occurs in confusion following Alexander's death. Leaders are Russian noblemen who were with army in Paris or traveled in Europe and resolved that Russia should have a constitution. Nicholas I crushes them brutally, persecutes students, etc. Educated begin to sympathize with rebels.

1853–1856
Crimean War. Russians surrender at Sevastopol, give up Bessarabia and other European territory, turn toward Asia for trade, land.

1820–1837
Golden Age of Russian Poetry: Pushkin, Lermontov, Tyutchev.

1840–1877

Golden Age of Russian Prose: Lermontov, Gogol, Goncharov, Turgenev, Dostoevsky, Tolstoy.

1861

Alexander II emancipates serfs. Gradually a social change had been occurring, a young intelligentsia (middle class as well as noble) rising, a social consciousness (documented by poet-journalist Nikolai Nekrasov, particularly concerned with suffering of peasants, and by Turgenev), a new concern for science. Youth began to form secret revolutionary societies: The Nihilists, led by the violent Nechaev; The Extremists, their anarchism based on Bakunin's theories; *Zemlya i Volya,* whose peasants and intellectuals joined for freedom and the communal ownership of property.

1862

The Communist Manifesto by Karl Marx translated into Russian.

1872

Das Kapital circulated in Russia.

1881

Alexander II assassinated by *Norodo Volya,* a branch of *Zemlya i Volya,* which had split in 1879.

1894–1912

Arts flourish: Stanislavsky and the Moscow Art Theater; Diaghilev and the Ballet Russe (brought to Paris in 1909); Mussorgsky, Borodin, Rimsky-Korsakov, Tchaikovsky, Stravinsky make St. Petersburg the center of music; also, The Silver Age of Literature—Chekhov, Gorky, Andreyev, Bunin, and Blok.

1898

Russian Social Democratic Labor Party formed on Marxist theories.

1903

Party splits into Marxists, non-Marxists. Non-Marxists (like *Volya*) applaud terrorism, form Socialist Revolutionary Party. Marxists divide into Bolsheviks ("majority") and Mensheviks ("minority"). Lenin becomes leader of Bolsheviks.

1905

Russo-Japanese war, Russia defeated. "Bloody Sunday": 1500 peaceful demonstrators slaughtered by czar's troops. Strikes which paralyze industry follow. Manifesto for freedom granted October 17; first Duma (parliament) organized.

206

1914–1918
World War I. Russia joins England, France, in Triple Entente.

1917
Riots in St. Petersburg, Nicholas II and Alexandra taken prisoner after abdication, murdered months later. Czarist rule ends.

1918
"March Revolution" leads to Kerensky's provisional government, a Socialist Revolutionary majority. "October Revolution" overthrows it, Bolsheviks under Lenin form Communist dictatorship. Moscow supplants St. Petersburg as capital. Treaty of Brest-Litovsk with Germany; loss of European territories—Finland, Estonia, Latvia, Lithuania, Poland, the Ukraine become independent states. Many patriotic Russians indignant.

1919
Civil War, Reds versus Whites (anti-Bolsheviks).

1922
USSR, a federal union of soviets, established. Russian republic is supreme in influence. Theaters of Meyerhold, Tairov flower.

1924
Lenin dies. Stalin begins rise to power, purges his enemies.

1928
First Five-Year Plan. Sholokhov, Alexey Tolstoy, Pautovsky, Babel.

1929
Stalin becomes dictator. Reign of terror intensified by secret police under Beria.

1932
Union of Soviet Writers formed; doctrine of socialist realism and central control of literature.

1939
Nazi-Soviet Pact. Nazis invade Poland. World War II begins. USSR takes back Estonia, Latvia, Lithuania, Bessarabia, rights to Gulf of Finland.

1941
Nazis invade Russia. Allies (England, France, United States) join to defend Russia. Siege of Leningrad. Moscow threatened.

207

1943
Battle of Stalingrad; tide turned toward victory of 1945.

1945
Yalta conference; Russia promises to aid Allies in Asian war. Hiroshima ends war. Communist-ruled "satellites" in Eastern Europe: Albania, Bulgaria, Hungary, Poland, Rumania, East Germany.

1948
Only Tito and Yugoslavia resist, expelled from Cominform. Czechoslovakia added to satellites. Iron Curtain drops. Cold War starts as East and West distrust each other. Blockade of West Berlin.

1950
Understanding with China as communism spreads there.

1953
Stalin dies. Beria falls. Krushchev begins rise to power.

1956
Twentieth Congress of the Party hears Krushchev's speech exposing Stalin, outlining his crimes. De-Stalinization under way; relaxation of censorship; Ehrenburg's *The Thaw* gives period a name.

1962
Solzhenitsyn's *One Day in the Life of Ivan Denisovitch* startles readers. Public poetry readings again popular.

1963
Manège exhibit of abstract and experimental art denounced by Krushchev; young writers and artists feel chill; socialist realism still the policy.

1964
Fall of Krushchev. Disputes with Communist China increasing.

1968
Invasion of Czechoslovakia. Solzhenitsyn's novels *The First Circle, Cancer Ward,* published in the West, lead to his Nobel Prize of 1970.

Title Index